THE

GOVERNMENT OF OHIO,

ITS HISTORY, RESOURCES AND JURISPRUDENCE,

ALSO, A BRIEF OUTLINE OF THE

GOVERNMENT OF THE UNITED STATES,

FOR THE USE OF
COLLEGES, HIGH SCHOOLS, GRAMMAR SCHOOLS,
AND GENERAL READERS,

BY CHARLES R. BROWN.

PUBLISHED BY MOORE & QUALE,
KALAMAZOO, MICHIGAN.

PRINTED BY KALAMAZOO PUBLISHING COMPANY.
1875.

TABLE OF CONTENTS

HISTORY OF OHIO.

GOVERNMENT AND LAW.

LEGISLATIVE DEPARTMENT.

EXECUTIVE DEPARTMENT.

BENEVOLENT, PENAL AND REFORMATORY INSTITUTIONS.

CRIMES AND MISDEMEANORS.

REVENUES OF THE STATE.

REAL ESTATE AND PERSONAL PROPERTY.

DOMESTIC RELATIONS.

SUNDRY MATTERS AFFECTING CIVIL RIGHTS.

GOVERNMENT OF THE UNITED STATES.

TO TEACHERS AND PUPILS.

The object of this work is to supply a want long felt and now fully recognized by the people. Books have been written on the science of government, which have gained admittance into our schools; and many of our youth have, in this way, acquired much valuable information. They have learned some of the first lessons of civil government, and have been made acquainted with the outline of the government, and perhaps history of the United States, but as yet they have not been supplied with that information concerning our own State, so important to enable them to discharge their duties as citizens.

If we would be true to ourselves, true to society, and true to the State, we must study to know what are the rights, privileges and duties of the citizen.

Dr. Lord, in his *Old Roman World*, says: "If the Romans had bequeathed nothing but laws to posterity, they would not have lived in vain. These have more powerfully affected the interests of civilization than the arts of Greece."

If, during the golden age of Roman jurisprudence it was disgraceful for a patrician and a noble to be ignorant of the law with which he had to do, what shall we say of those who, ignorant of the laws of the commonwealth, attempt to govern the people and to legislate for them.

It is the theory of our government that merit is the citizen's guarantee of success; that *worth*—not *wealth*—makes the man; that moral and intellectual fitness—not heriditary honors—give to our countrymen place and power, and assign to our citizens their proper sphere in the civil, political and religious circles.

We should always bear in mind that we are American citizens, and as such have in our keeping the institutions transmitted to us by the heroes of '76, as an inheritance more precious than the world's wealth; an inheritance that must not be permitted to deteriorate, but that must be protected, improved and cultivated by wise stateman-ship, so that our institutions shall continue to shed their luster, and demonstrate to the world that freedom rather than tyrany liberty rather than despotism shall triumph. This duty we owe, not to ourselves and our posterity only, but to the victims of despotic arogance in the old world—to the oppressed of every clime—who are invited to share in the immunities guaranteed to us in the *magna charta* of our liberties.

In introducing to the public The Government of Ohio, the author entertains the hope that its pages will be found to embrace information tending to fit and prepare the student to discharge faithfully and well the duties of citizenship, and to strengthen his attachment and increase his love for the institutions of the country.

In preparing the chapters relating to the early history of the State, the author has had access to various documents and histories. Among these the *Ohio Historical Collections*, by Henry Howe, Esq., of Cincinnati—a work that should be in the hands of every citizen—has been found most valuable.

GOVERNMENT OF OHIO.

HISTORY OF OHIO.

CHAPTER I.

OHIO, ORIGIN OF THE NAME—EXPLORATIONS AND LABORS OF THE FRENCH JESUITS IN THE NORTHWESTERN TERRITORY.

Ohio derives its name from the river constituting its southern boundary. Col. John Johnson who, many years ago, was the agent of the United States Government to the Indians, furnished for *Howe's Historical Collections* the following in reference to the origin and signification of the name Ohio:

"Ohio may be called an improvement on the expression, *O, he zuh*, and was no doubt adopted by the early French voyagers in their boat songs, and is substantially the same word as used by the Wyandots; the meaning applied by the French, fair and beautiful, '*la belle rivere*' being precisely the same as meant by the Indians—great, grand and fair to look upon."

The territory northwest of the Ohio river was partially explored by some French explorers as early as the year 1610. In 1632, Father Sagard visited the country along the shores of Lake Huron. In 1634, a party of Indians belonging to the Huron tribe visited Quebec, a walled city in Canada. On their return they were accompanied by the Jesuits, Breboeuf and Daniel, who located upon the shore of Lake Iroquois, a bay of Lake Huron, and instructed the natives in religious matters.

In 1641 a number of French Jesuits paddled a bark canoe from the St. Lawrence river up through the Ottawa river thence crossing over to Lake Nipissing, thence down the French river to the Georgian Bay, and passing the islands of Lake Huron, they reached the Falls of St. Mary, where they established a Mission.

In 1660, Rene Mesnard attempted an exploration of the territory around Green Bay and Lake Superior. In October of that year, he reached a bay on the south shore of Lake Superior, which he called St. Theresa. After remaining there for about eight months, he was lost in the forest. His breviary and cassock were subsequently discovered among the amulets of the Sioux, by whom he was probably murdered.

In 1666, Father Allouez established a mission at the Falls of St. Mary, now called Sault Ste. Marie, where, in 1668, he was joined by Fathers Dablon and Marquette. In the course of the next three years they explored the country along the shores of Lake Michigan, making the entire circuit of that lake. In 1671, Marquette built a chapel at Mackinaw, formerly called Michilimackinac, also Mackinac.

In 1673, Father Marquette and Joliet sailed through the Straits of Mackinaw on their way to discover the

Mississippi. They were followed, six years later, by Robert de la Salle, who built and navigated the *Griffin*, a bark of sixty tons burden—the first vessel that ever floated on the northwestern lakes. The *Griffin* had on board Louis Hennepin, the missionary, and a party of fur-traders, who landed at Michilimackinac, and erected a fort and established a trading post.

Questions—From what did Ohio derive its name? In what year was the country nowest of the Ohio river partially explored? Give the dates and particulars of the visits of Sagard, Brebœuf and Daniel. State what was done by certain French Jesuits in 1641. What is said of Rene Mesnard? Of Allouez, Dablon and Marquette? Of Marquette and Joliet? Of de la Salle and those who companied him?

CHAPTER II.

FRENCH MISSIONARIES AND TRADERS—ESTABLISHMENT OF MILITARY AND TRADING POSTS—SURRENDER OF THE TERRITORY TO THE ENGLISH—THE PONTIAC WAR.

In the fall of 1679, LaSalle and his men went to Green Bay and procured a cargo of furs and dispatched them in the Griffin for Niagara. But the vessel was lost on the voyage.

From Michilimackinac, LaSalle and fourteen of his men paddled their canoes up Lake Michigan to the mouth of the St. Joseph river, where they erected a rude fort.

In July, 1701, Antoine de la Cadillac, with a Jesuit

missionary and one hundred men, located at the present site of Detroit, and commenced a permanent settlement. Here they erected a stockade which they named Fort Ponchertrain.

The forts erected at Green Bay, Ste. Marie, St. Joseph, Michilimackinac, Fort Gratiot, Detroit, at the mouth of the Wabash, and other points, were designed as outposts by which the claim of the French to govern the territory could be suppported, and the traders and missionaries be protected.

In 1748, the Ohio Company was formed, and attempted to establish trading houses among the Indians.

In 1749, the English built a trading house upon the Great Miami, a place since called Laramie's Store. This house was destroyed by the French, assisted by the Ottowa and Chippewa Indians. This trading post is supposed to have been the first British settlement in the Ohio Valley.

In 1756, Major Lewis was sent with a party of troops against the Indian towns on the Ohio.

Prior to 1760, France claimed all of Canada and borders of the Mississippi, while the English occupied most of the country east of the Alleghany Mountains. The English, however, claimed dominion west of the Alleghanies, on the alleged ground that the Six Nations owned the Ohio Valley and had placed it under the protection of England.

The Six Nations was composed of six tribes of Indians: the Onondagas, Cayugas, Oneidas, Senecas, Mohawks, and Tuscororas.

Both countries desired supremacy over the northern

portion of the New World, and a fierce struggle between them ensued. In November, 1760, Detroit, Michilimackinac, and all the posts within the government of Canada, that were in possession of the French, were surrendered to the Crown of England.

While some of the Indians cheerfully acquiesced in the change from the rule of the French to that of the English, a large proportion of them were dissatisfied, and still retained a strong friendship for the French government; and in the month of May, 1763, a simultaneous attack was made upon the forts of LeBœuf, Venango, Presque Isle, Michilimackinac, St. Joseph, Miama, Green Bay, Ouiatonon, Pittsburgh, Sandusky, Niagara and Detroit. This attack resulted in a most frightful massacre at each of these points; Detroit, Pittsburgh and Niagara being the only places that did not fall into the hands of the savages.

Pontiac, an Ottawa chief who lived on Pechee Island, about eight miles above the city of Detroit, was at this time the most prominent and influential leader among the Indians. Hence this war is known in history as the Pontiac War.

The seige of Detroit by Pontiac continued for eleven months, when the post was relieved by Gen. Bradstreet, with an army of three thousand men.

Questions.—What is said of LaSalle and his men? Of Antoine de la Cadillac and the Jesuit missionaries? For what purpose were the forts at the different points erected? What is said of the Ohio Company? Of the English trading house? What occurred in 1756? Prior to 1760 what territory was claimed by France? What was occupied by the English? What claim was made by the English? What occurred in 1760? In 1763? What is said of Pontiac? Of the siege of Detroit?

CHAPTER III.

INDIAN HOSTILITIES—CONFLICTS, BATTLES AND TREATIES WITH THE INDIANS FROM 1764 TO 1788—MORAVIAN MISSIONARIES AND INDIANS.

In 1764, General Bradstreet passed from Detroit into the Wyandot country, ascending the Sandusky bay in boats, where a treaty of peace was effected with the Indians. The Shawnees, of the Scioto river, and the Delawares, of the Muskingum river, however, continued their hostilities. Col. Bouquet, however, shortly afterward succeeded in entering into a treaty of peace with the hostile Indians, who restored the prisoners they had captured.

Prior to the war of the Revolution, the Moravian missionaries had a number of missionary stations within the present limits of Ohio. In March, 1782, a party of Americans, under Col. Williamson, murdered 94 of the Moravian Indians within the present limits of Tuscarawas county. In the June following, Col. Crawford at head of about five hundred men, was defeated by the Indians, three miles north of the site of Upper Sandusky. The The Colonel was taken prisoner and burnt at the stake, with horrible tortures.

During the war of the Revolution, the Indians of the Northwestern Territory were induced to make war upon the American settlements in New York, Pennsylvania, and Virginia.

Early in 1774, the Indians again became troublesome

and committed depredations upon the white settlements.

The settlers built block houses, or forts, of logs, in which they were frequently compelled to take refuge to defend themselves against the savages. During this year (1774) an expedition under Col. McDonald attacked the Indians and destroyed the Indian town of Wapatomica. This town was situated a few miles above the present site of Zanesville.

Block House, near North Bend.

In the following fall the Indians were defeated at Point Pleasant, on the Virginia side of the Ohio river. Soon after this, Lord Dunmore met the Indians at Camp Charlotte, in what is now Pickaway county, and made peace with them.

In 1779, Col. Bowman marched against the Shawnees, but was forced to retreat.

In 1780, General Broadhead marched against the Indian towns in the forks of the Muskingum. This expedition was called the Coshocton Campaign. During the same year, General Clark, with a body of Kentuckians, marched against the Shawnees and defeated them at Piqua, on Mad river, six miles below the present site of Springfield.

In 1782, Gen. Clark led a second expedition against the Shawnees and destroyed their towns, Upper and Lower Piqua, on the Miami.

In 1786, Col. Logan fought the Indians successfully in what is now Logan county.

In 1787, Col. Edwards led an expedition to the headwaters of the Big Miami, and in 1788 Tod led one into the Scioto Valley.*

Questions—What is said in the first paragraph of this lesson in relation to treaties of peace? Of the Moravian missionaries and Indians? Of Col. Crawford? What is said of the conduct of the Indians during the Revolutionary war? What occurred early in 1774? What occurred in the fall of that year? What occurred in 1779? In 1780? In 1782? In 1786? In 1787? In 1788?

CHAPTER IV.

THE ENGLISH LAND GRANTS—COLONIAL CHARTERS—CLAIMS OF NEW YORK, CONNECTICUT, MASSACHUSETTS AND VIRGINIA.

In the early history of the country, questions involv-

*Hist. Col. of Ohio, by Howe, p. 8.

ing the title to the territory were not always adjusted without difficulty. The different European powers claimed large portions of the territory on the ground of the first discoveries made by their subjects.

In 1609 the English monarch granted to the London Company all the territory extending along the coast for two hundred miles, north and south, from Point Comfort, and "up into the land, throughout, from sea to sea, west and northwest." This company was dissolved by a decree of the court, in 1624, and the grant was resumed by the government.

In 1662, Charles II. granted to certain settlers upon the Connecticut, all the territory between the parallels of latitude which include the present State of Connecticut, from the Atlantic to the Pacific ocean. The pretensions which Massachusetts advanced, during the Revolutionary war, to to an interest in the western country were founded upon a similar charter granted thirty years afterwards.*

In the treaty of peace of 1783, at the close of the Revolutionary war, there was no express stipulation for the surrender of the northwestern posts, although the territory embracing them was clearly embraced within the treaty. Notwithstanding this, the British government continued in possession of them until 1796.

Included in the grants of territory to the various companies, by England, were certain powers of government; and out of these grants colonies were organized with charters specifying what governmental powers might be exercised.

---

*Holmes' Annals, i., 436.

After the Declaration of Independence in 1776, the new States claimed the right of soil and jurisdiction over the district of country embraced in their colonial charters, notwithstanding the British Government had assumed to revoke these grants.

Some of these charters embraced large portions of western lands, and the States which had no such charters claimed that these lands ought by right to be disposed of for the common benefit of all the States, according to their population, inasmuch as the title to them would be secured, if at all, by the united efforts and sacrifices of all the States.

The State of Virginia, in March, 1784, ceded the right of soil and jurisdiction to the district of country embraced in her charter, situated to the northwest of the river Ohio.

In September, 1786, the State of Connecticut also ceded her claim of soil and *jurisdiction* to the district of country within the limits of her charter, situated west of a line beginning at the completion of the forty-first point degree of north latitude, one hundred and twenty miles west of the western boundary of Pennsylvania, and from thence by a line drawn north parallel to, and one hundred and twenty miles west of said line of Pennsylvania, and to continue north until it comes to forty-two degrees and two minutes north latitude. The State of Connecticut on the 30th of May, 1801, also ceded her jurisdictional claims to all that territory called the "Western Reserve of Connecticut."*

The States of New York and Massachusetts had

*Howe's His. Col., 9. See also Chase's Sketch of the History of Ohio, 14.

already ceded their claims without making any reservations.

Treaties were subsequently made with the Indians who were in reality the rightful owners of the soil, whereby their title was extinguished.

The first permanent English settlement in Ohio, was made April 7th, 1788, at Marietta; and the first judicial court was held there in September of the same year under an act of Congress passed in 1786. The next settlement was that of Symmes' purchase, six miles below Cincinnati, in 1789. The next was made by French emigrants, at Gallipolis, in 1791. The next was made on Lake Erie, at Cleveland and Conneaut, in 1796, by emigrants from New England. In 1799, the first territorial legislature met at Cincinnati, and organized the government.

Questions.—What claim was made, in the early history of the country, by European powers? What grant was made by the English monarch in 1609? What grant was made in 1662? What is said of the treaty of 1783? Of the colonial charters? What claim was made by certain States after the Revolution? By others? What was done by Virginia in March, 1784? By Connecticut in September, 1786? In May, 1801? What had New York and Massachusetts done previous to this, in regard to the territory claimed by them? What is said of treaties made after 1801? When and where was the first permanent settlement in Ohio made? The first court held? Subsequent settlements? What occurred in 1799?

CHAPTER V.

THE ORDINANCE OF 1787.

In 1787, Congress adopted the celebrated ordinance for the government of the Northwestern Territory. This ordinance provided for the descent of property and for the disposition thereof by deed or will; saving, however, to the French and Canadian inhabitants, and other settlers of the Kaskaskies, St. Vincents and the neighboring villages who had professed themselves citizens of Virginia, their laws and customs then in force among them relative to the descent and conveyance of property.

It provided for the appointment of a governor and secretary, by Congress, and for the establishment of a court, to consist of three judges with *common law jurisdiction.*

The ordinance provided that the governor and judges, or a majority of them should adopt and publish in the district such laws in the original States as should be necessary and best suited to the circumstances of the district, and to report them to Congress from time to time. These laws were to continue in force until the organization of the General Assembly, unless disapproved of by Congress.

The governor was made, by virtue of his office, commander-in-chief of the militia. He was required to appoint magistrates and other civil officers, and to subdivide the district in which the Indian titles had been extinguished, into counties and townships.

It fixed the basis of representation and prescribed the qualifications of electors.

It provided for the organization of the General Assembly so soon as there should be five thousand free male inhabitants, of full age, in the district, and for the election of a delegate to Congress.

The ordinance contained six articles of compact embodying the genuine principles of freedom and the true theory of American liberty. In short, they were designed, as the ordinance declares, "to extend the fundamental principles of civil and religious liberty which forms the basis whereon these republics, their laws and constitutions are erected; to fix and establish those principles as the basis of all laws, constitutions and governments which forever, hereafter, shall be formed in said territory; to provide also for the establishment of States and permanent governments therein, and for their admission to a share in the federal councils on an equal footing with the original States, at as early periods as may be consistent with the general interest."

The first article provided that no person demeaning himself in a peaceable and orderly manner should ever be molested on account of his mode of worship or religious sentiments.

The second guaranteed to all the inhabitants the benefits of the writ of *habeas corpus*, and of trial by jury, of judicial proceedings according to the course of the common law, and of a representative government. It also prohibited legislative interference with private contracts. No person was to be deprived of his liberty or property but by the judgment of his peers or the law of the land,

and no private property or services should be taken or demanded for public use without full compensation.

The third required the government to encourage schools, and to observe the utmost good faith toward the Indians. It recognized religion, morality, and knowledge as being necessary to good government and the happiness of mankind.

The fourth and fifth articles related to the formation of new States within the Territory, and their admission into the Union. The navigable tributaries of the Mississipi and the St. Lawrence, with the portages between the same, were established as common highways, and forever free to all the citizens of the United States.

The sixth and last article declared that there should be neither slavery nor involuntary servitude within the Territory, otherwise than in the punishment of crimes, whereof the party shall have been duly convicted.

In referring to this ordinance, the late Chief Justice Chase said: "This remarkable instrument was the last gift of the Congress of the old Confederation to the country; and it was a fit consummation of their glorious labors."

Questions.—In what year did Congress adopt the ordinance for the government of the Northwestern Territory? What did the ordinance provide with reference to property? Governor and court? With reference to laws? Mention some of the duties required of the governor? What of representation and of electors? Of the General Assembly and representation in Congress? How many articles of compact did the ordinance contain? What did they embody? For what purposes were they designed? What does the first article of the compact provide? The second? The third? The fourth? The fifth? The sixth? What did the late Chief Justice Chase say of this ordinance?

CHAPTER VI.

MISSIONARY WORK IN OHIO—PIONEER CHURCHES.

At a very early day the French Jesuits established missions in the territory northwest of the Ohio, an account of which is given in a preceeding chapter.

In 1761, Frederick Post, a Moravian Missionary, established a mission in what is now Bethlehem Township, Stark County, on the north side of the Muskingum at the junction of the Sandy and Tuscarawas.

In 1771-2 the Moravian Missionaries established missions at Shoenbrun, Gnadenhutten and Salem, on the Tuscarawas river, within the limits of the present county of Tuscarawas.

About ten years after the establishment of these missions, several depradations were committed by hostile Indians on the inhabitants of Western Pennsylvania and Virginia. A company of militia was raised for the purpose of retaliating, and under the command of Col. Williamson, marched against the Moravian Indians on the Tuscarawas, who had been guilty of no wrong, and massacred over ninety of their number.

Feeling the influence of public sympathy in behalf of those persecuted people, and recognizing the power of their teachings as an agent of civilization, Congress, in 1788 donated 12,000 acres of land to the Moravian Society, embracing the three villages already mentioned, for propagating the gospel among the heathen.

In 1791, Rev. James Kemper was escorted by a delegation from the first Presbyterian society of Cincinnati, "from beyond the Kentucky river to Cincinnati; and after his arrival a subscription was set on foot" to build the church shown by the engraving. This subscription paper bears date January 16, 1792, the same year in which the church was erected. In the spring of '47 the building was taken down and the material used in the construction of dwellings in that part of Cincinnati called Texas.

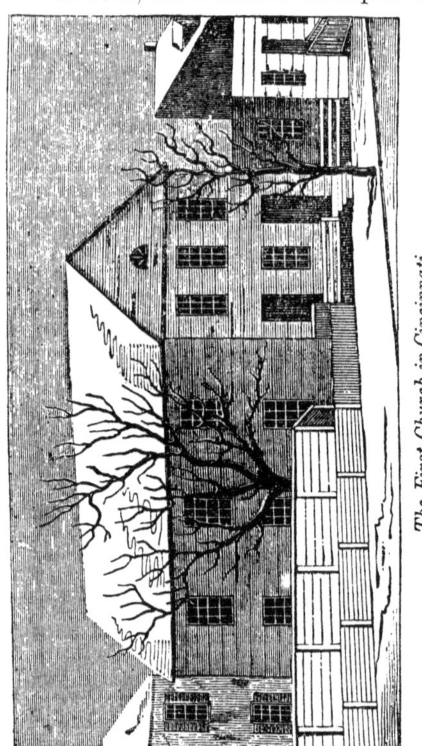

The First Church in Cincinnati.

In 1776, Zeisberger, a Moravian Missionary, with a band of Indian converts, came from Detroit to the mouth of the Cuyahoga in a vessel called the Mackinaw, and located on the river about ten miles above the present site of Cleveland, at a place which they named *Pilgerruh*, *i. e. Pilgrim's Rest.* The pagan Indians compelled them, after a few months, to leave. From there they went to the Huron river, and commenced a settlement on the east bank, to which they gave the name of New Salem. The persecutions of the Indians, however, soon compelled them to abandon this place.

In 1804, Christian Frederick Dencke, a Moravian Missionary, established a mission at an Indian village called Petquatting, where Milan now stands. The mission was abandoned in 1809.

The first Indian mission formed by the Methodists in the Mississippi Valley was at Upper Sandusky. John Stewart, a mulatto, commenced preaching at that place in 1816. A few years later a church was organized and a school established, under the direction of Rev. James B. Finley. "The mission church building was erected of blue limestone about the year 1824, from government funds, Finley having permission from

Wyandot Mission Church, at Upper Sandusky.

Hon. John C. Calhoun, then Secretary of War, to apply $1,300 to this object. Connected with the mission was a school house, and a farm of one mile square"—640 acres.*

Questions—What mission was established in 1761? In 1771-2? What is said of the massacre of the Moravian Indians? What action was taken by Congress? What is said of the first church at Cincinnati? Of Zeisberger and the missions established by him? Of Dencke? Of the mission at Upper Sandusky?

CHAPTER VII.

STRUGGLES WITH THE INDIANS—ORGANIZATION OF COUNTIES—NAMING OF CINCINNATI—ORGAIZATION OF THE FIRST TERRITORIAL LEGISLATURE—ADMISSION OF THE STATE INTO THE UNION.

In the year 1789, the Indians, who for a number of years had been peaceably disposed, engaged in acts of hostility toward the white settlers near the mouth of the Muskingum and between the Miamis,† and in the month of June of that year Major Dougherty constructed Fort Washington, at the present site of Cincinnati. Soon after, General Harmer, with three hundred men, took command of the fort.

---

*His. Col. of Ohio, by Howe.
†The Maumee river was formerly called the Miami of the Lake.

CINCINNATI IN 1810.

In September, 1790, with thirteen hundred men, Gen. Harmer marched against the savages, but was defeated. About one-fourth of his force were regular soldiers and the rest consisted of militia. All the regulars except nine, and more than a hundred of the militia were killed. Soon after this, Governor St. Clair, with a force of two thousand three hundred regulars and about six hundred militia, marched against the Indians. He was, however, unsuccessful, and General Butler and upward of six hundred men were killed.

In the spring of 1794, the American army, under the command of General Anthony Wayne, assembled at Greenville, in what is now Darke county. This army consisted of about two thousand regular troops and fifteen hundred mounted volunteers from Kentucky. On the 20th of August of that year, Wayne met the Indians at the foot of the rapids of the Maumee, a short distance south of the present site of Maumee City, and after a short and deadly conflict defeated them. Shortly after this a treaty of peace was made at Greenville.

In 1788 Washington county was formed, being the first organized within the limits of Ohio. It was bounded as follows: "Beginning on the bank of the Ohio river where the western boundary line of Pennsylvania crosses it, and running with that line to Lake Erie; thence along the southern shore of said lake to the mouth of the Cuyahoga river; thence up said river to the portage between it and the Tuscarawas branch of the Muskingum; thence down that branch to the forks at the crossing place above Fort Laurens; thence with a line to be drawn westerly to the portage on that branch of the Big Miami on which the fort stood that was taken by the French in 1752, until it meets the road from the lower Shawnese town to Sandusky; thence south to the Scioto river, and thence with that river to the mouth, and thence up the Ohio river to the place of beginning."

In 1790, the county of Hamilton was erected, and included the country between the Miamis extending northward from the Ohio river to a line drawn due east from the standing stone forks of the great Miami,* and about the same time the name of the settlement opposite the mouth of the Licking was changed by Gov. St. Clair from Losantiville to Cincinnati, in honor of the military society of Cincinnati, then recently organized, of which the governor and several other early emigrants were members.†

The third county formed in the Northwest Territory was the county of Wayne. This was in 1796. This county embraced all the northwestern part of Ohio, Indiana, Illinois, Wisconsin, and all of Michigan.

Adams county was formed July 10th, 1797, and embraced within its limits a large tract lying on both sides of the Scioto.

Before the end of the year 1798, four new counties were carved out of those already established, thus making eight in all, with a population of five thousand free male inhabitants over twenty-one years of age.

By the terms of the ordinance of 1787, the people were now (1798) authorized to elect representatives to a territorial legislature, and on the 24th day of September, 1799, the first territorial legislature was organized. This legislature elected William H. Harrison as delegate to Congress.

---

*Terr. Local Laws. †Chase's Sketch of Ohio, 25.

November 1st, 1802, a convention assembled at Chillicothe to frame a constitution for a State government, and on the 29th of that month the constitution for a State government was ratified and signed by the members of the convention, and Ohio became one of the States of the Federal Union, February 19th, 1803.

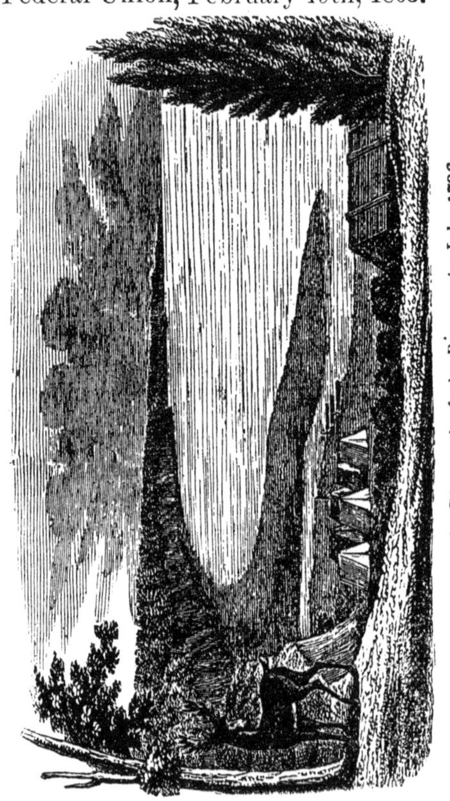

Conneaut, the Plymouth of the Reserve, in July. 1796.*

On the 4th of July, 1796, the first surveying party of the Western Reserve, landed at the mouth of Conneaut creek, in what is now Ashtabula county. John Barr, Esq., in his sketch of the Western Reserve, published in the *National Magazine* for December, 1845, referring to this party, says:

"Mustering their numbers, they sat them down on the eastward shore of the stream now known as Con-

*The word Conneaut, in the language of the Seneca Indians, signifies "*many fish*," and was applied originally to the river.

neaut, and, dipping from the lake the liquor in which they pledged their country—their goblets some *tin cups* of no rare workmanship, yet every way answerable, with the ordnance accompaniment of two or three fowling pieces, discharging the required national salute—the first settlers of the Reserve spent their landing-day as became the sons of the Pilgrim Fathers—as the advance pioneers of a population that has since made the wilderness of northern Ohio to 'blossom as the rose,' and prove the homes of a people as remarkable for integrity, industry, love of country, moral truth and enlightened legislation, as any to be found within the territorial limits of their ancestral New England.

"The whole party numbered fifty-two persons."

Questions—What transpired in 1789 with reference to the Indians? State the particulars of the campaign against the Indians in 1790. Of Governor St. Clair's expedition. Of Gen. Wayne's. Give the name, date of organization, and boundaries of the first county in the Northwest Territory. Of the second. Give the date and particulars concerning the naming of Cincinnati. Give the name, date of organization, and territory of the third county. Of the fourth. What was the population of the Northwestern Territory in 1798? When was the first Territorial Legislature organized, and who did it elect as delegate to Congress? When and where did the covention assemble to adopt a State constitution? When was the constitution signed and ratified by the convention? What is said of the first settlement of the Western Reserve?

THE LOG CABIN.

There are, doubtless, those who have never seen a log cabin, and who know nothing of the hardships and trials of pioneer life.

Our Cabin; or Life in the Woods

Our engraving represents the cabin in which John S. Williams, Esq., late editor of the *American Pioneer*, was reared. It was constructed on Glenn's Run, about six miles northeast of St. Clairsville, Belmont county.

While the design and scope of this work will not justify anything like a history of pioneer life, the author deems it proper to remind the student that in view of the trials and perils through which our ancestors have passed, we should cherish their memory with gratitude, and strive to prove ourselves worthy of the grand inheritance transmitted to us.

The following discription of the cabin shown in the engraving, will serve to describe most of the dwellings of the pioneers of Ohio: "Our cabin was 18x24. The west end was occupied by two beds, the center of each side by a door; and here our symmetry had to stop, for on the opposite side of the window, made of clapboards, supported on pins driven into the logs, were our shelves. A ladder of five rounds occupied the corner near the window. The window was made by sawing out a log, placing sticks across, and then, by pasting an old newspaper over the hole, and applying some hog's lard, we had a kind of glazing which shed a *most beautiful and mellow light* across the cabin. Our chimney occupied most of the east end."

CHAPTER VIII.

THE OLD STATE HOUSE—TERRITORIAL AND STATE LEGISLATURES —LOCATION OF THE CAPITAL—THE WAR OF 1812.

In 1800, Congress passed an act removing the seat of government of the Northwest Territory from Cincinnati to Chillicothe.

The old state house was commenced in 1800 and finished in 1801-2. "It is believed that it was the first public stone edifice erectin the Territory. The mason work was done by Major Wm. Rutledge, a soldier of the Revolution, and the carpentering by William Guthrie. The convention that framed the constitution of Ohio was held in it

Old State House, Chillicothe.

in 1802. In 1803, the first General Assembly of the State met in the house, and held their sessions there until 1810. The sessions of 1810–11 and 1811–12 were held at Zanesville, and from there removed back to Chillicothe and held in this house until 1816, when Columbus became the permanent capital of the State."*

The General Assembly, in 1803, elected the first State officers, as follows: Michael Baldwin, speaker of the house of representatives; Nathaniel Massie, speaker of the senate; William Creighton, Jr., secretary of state; Col. Thomas Gibson, auditor; William McFarland, treasurer; Return J. Meigs, Jr., Samuel Huntington, and William Sprigg, judges of the supreme court; Francis Dunlary, Wyllys Silliman, and Calvin Pease, judges of the district courts.

In 1810, the Indians, who since the treaty of peace at Greenville had been peaceable, influenced by the British, whose intention it was to prevent the further extension of the settlements, again commenced their aggressions upon the inhabitants, and in 1811 General Harrison, then governor of the Indian territory, marched against the Indians upon the Wabash. The Indians were under the command of a brother of the celebrated Tecumseh, called "the Prophet." The battle of Tippecanoe followed, in what is now Cass county, Indiana, and the Indians were defeated.

In 1812, war was declared between the United States and Great Britain. The chief causes of this war were the impressment of American seamen, the capture of Amer-

*American Pioneer, and Howe's Hist. Col.

ican vessels, and the enforcement of illegal blockades by the English government.

On the 12th of July, 1812, General Hull, in command at Detroit, surrendered to the British under General Brock. General Harrison soon after sent General Winchester into Michigan at the head of a thousand men, with a view to the recapture of Detroit. January 19, 1813, Winchester was attacked at Frenchtown, on the River Raisin, by the British General Proctor, with a force of two thousand British and Indians. Winchester was taken prisoner, and his entire detachment surrendered, Proctor assuring them that he would protect them from the savages. He, however, withdrew his troops to Malden, leaving his prisoners to be massacred by the Indians.

Though for a time defeat, disaster and disgrace was the fate of our forces, victory at last perched upon our banners.

On the 2d of August, 1813, Col. Croghan made a most gallant defense at Fort Stephenson, at Lower Sandusky, against an overwhelming force of British and Indians.

On the 10th of September of the same year, Commodore Perry defeated the British at the battle of Lake Erie; and on the 5th of October, General Harrison defeated the British and Indians at the battle of the Thames. At this battle, the renowned chief Tecumseh was in command of the Indian warriors, and fought with wonderful courage and desperation. After the British had fled, Tecumseh, with his Indian warriors, engaged in a hand-to-hand conflict with Colonel Johnson and his force of mounted Kentuckians, but soon fell pierced by a pistol ball. It is said that during the latter years of his life, "he was almost incessantly engaged either in council or at the head of his war-like bands," and that "he sank at last on the field of his glory, with tomahawk in hand and the cry of battle upon his lips."

" Like monumental bronze, unchanged his look,
A soul which pity touch'd, but never shook;
Train'd from his tree-rock'd cradle to his bier,
The fierce extremes of good and ill to brook;
Unchanging, fearing but the shame of fear,
A stoic of the woods, a man without a tear."

Immediately after the battle of the Thames, the British surrendered Detroit to the Americans, but retained the possession of Mackinac, in Michigan, until December 24, 1814, when negotiations for peace were concluded.

Questions.—In what year was the seat of government removed from Cincinnati to Chillicothe? What is said of the old state house? Of the Constitutional Convention? Of the meetings of the General Assembly from 1803 to 1816? Name the officers elected by the first General Assembly of the State. What is said with reference to the Indians in 1810 and 1811? With what foreign nation did the United States engage in war in 1812? State some of the chief causes of the war of 1812. When and to whom did General Hull surrender Detroit? State the particulars and result of General Winchester's campaign. What is said of General Crogan? When, by whom, and with what result was the battle of Lake Erie fought? Battle of the Thames? What is said of Tecumseh? When was peace declared?

CHAPTER IX.

COMMERCE AND FINANCE FROM 1814 TO 1820—BANKS AND BANKING—INTERNAL IMPROVEMENTS—EARLY LEGISLATION CONCERNING EDUCATION.

From the date of the treaty of peace between the United States and Great Britain, commercial intercourse was renewed, and excessive importations of foreign goods were made. The population of the State increased rapidly, and numerous banks were chartered which supplied an abundant circulating medium. Speculations naturally run to extravagant excesses, and many of the banks soon found themselves unable to redeem their paper.

In 1816, branches of the bank of the United States were established at Cincinnati and Chillicothe.

It is said that "these branches issued notes to a considerable amount, and the presence of this convertible paper doubtless tended to hasten the depreciation of the State currency. By receiving the notes of the State banks, also, until large quantities had been accumulated, and then calling on them to redeem their paper, the branch banks effectually tested the solvency of these institutions. Few could endure the ordeal.

"The notes of nearly all the local banks continued to sink lower and lower in the scale of depreciation, and the paper of several became absolutely worthless."*

* Chase's Hist. Sketch of Ohio, 42.

Many of the people were disposed to attribute their financial difficulties to the operations of the Bank of the United States, and in 1819 the General Assembly passed an act imposing an annual tax of fifty thousand dollars on each branch of the national bank established in the State. The banks refused to pay this tax and the collecting officer of the State entered the branch bank at Chillicothe, levied the tax upon specie and bank notes and deposited the proceeds in the State treasury at Columbus, ~~that city having been established as the seat of the State government in 1816~~.

The right of the State to tax banks created by act of Congress was immediately tested in the United States circuit court.

The case was finally taken to the supreme court of the United States, where a decision was rendered against the State.

In 1824 in pursuance of an act of the General Assembly, two lines of canal were located; one extending from the mouth of the Scioto to Coshocton and thence ~~by one of three different routes~~ to the lake, and another from Cincinnati to the foot of the rapids of the Maumee.

In 1825 a board of canal commissioners was authorized to commence the construction of canals from the mouth of the Scioto to the lake, and on so much of the Miami and Maumee line as lay between Cincinnati and Dayton.

The canal from the Ohio to the lake was called the Ohio canal; that from Cincinnati to Dayton, the Miami canal. These with other works of internal improvement subsequently constructed by the State, have had much to do in developing ~~our~~ resources.

In 1825 a uniform school system was established. A tax upon property of one half a mill upon the dollar for the support of schools was provided for.

In 1829 the school tax was increased to three-fourths of a mill upon the dollar, and provision was made for dividing the townships into districts.

In 1785 section sixteen in every township was set apart for the use of schools. This amounted to over seven hundred thousand acres. In the Ohio company's purchase two entire townships for a college were granted on which the "American Western University" was established. Its name was subsequently changed to the "Ohio University." In the Simms' purchase a township of land was granted for an academy. But as it was never located by the patentee, Congress gave another township in lieu of it which was located on the Great Miami, where the Miami University was established.

It will be seen that the General Assembly was not unmindful of the obligations of the ordinance of 1787, and that they recognized that religion, morality and knowledge are necessary to all good governments.

Questions—What is said in this lesson of the importation of goods and the establishment of banks? Of the establishment of branches of the bank of the United States? Of the notes issued by them? Of the notes of the local banks? What action was taken by the General Assembly in 1819? What was done by the collecting officer? What legal proceedings followed and what was the final result? What was done in 1824, towards making certain public improvements? In 1825? By what names were these canals called? What provision was made for promoting education in 1825? In 1829? What is said of section sixteen? Of the Ohio company's purchase? Of the Simms' purchase? Of the General Assembly and the ordinance of 1787?

CHAPTER X.

THE OHIO AND MICHIGAN, OR TOLEDO WAR.

By the ordinance of 1787, it was contemplated that a line due east and west through the southern extremity of Lake Michigan, should be the dividing line between the two tiers of States to be erected out of the Northwestern Territory.

On the 30th of April, 1802, Congress enacted a law "to enable the people of the eastern division of the territory northwest of the river Ohio, to form a constitution and State government, and for the admission of the same into the Union." The second section of that act is as follows: "That the said State shall consist of all the territory included within the following boundaries, to wit: bounded on the east by the Pennsylvania line, on the south by the Ohio river, to the mouth of the Great Miami, on the west by a line drawn due north from the mouth of the Great Miami aforesaid, and on the north by an east and west line drawn through the southerly extreme of Lake Michigan, running east, after intersecting the due north line aforesaid, from the mouth of the Great Miami, until it shall intersect Lake Erie, or the territorial line, and then with the same through Lake Erie to the Pennsylvania line aforesaid."

Pursuant to this act, a constitutional convention was called and a constitution framed. The article prescribing the boundaries of the State was in the language of the section above recited, but is followed by the following:

"Provided always, and it is hereby fully and expressly declared by this convention, that if the southerly bend or extreme of Lake Michigan should extend so far south that a line drawn due east from it should not intersect Lake Erie, or if it should intersect the said Lake Erie, east of the line of the mouth of the Miami river of the Lake, [now called the Maumee] then and in that case, *with the assent of the Congress of the United States*, the northern boundary of this State shall be established by, and extended to a direct line running from the southern extremity of Lake Michigan, to the most northerly cape of the Miami [Maumee] Bay, after intersecting the due north line from the mouth of the Great Miami river as aforesaid, thence northeast to the territorial line, and by the said territorial line to the Pennsylvania line."

Although Ohio was admitted into the Union under this constitution, Congress did not, in terms, assent to the *proviso* as to boundary; but, on the contrary, in 1805, clearly *dissented*, by organizing Michigan as a separate territory, fixing as its southern boundary the line contemplated by the ordinance of 1787.

In 1807, the General Assembly of Ohio passed a resolution instructing her senators and representatives in Congress to use their influence to obtain the passage of a law to ascertain and define the northern boundary line of this State, and fix the same agreeable to the proviso.

In 1812, the Surveyor-General of the United States caused two lines to be run, one in conformity with the enabling act of Congress, and the other as called for by the proviso. The line claimed by Michigan was called the Fulton line, and that claimed by Ohio was called the Harris line.

Notwithstanding the protests of Ohio, Michigan continued to exercise jurisdiction over the disputed territory, without serious opposition, until 1834 or 1835, though the court of common pleas of Wood county, soon after its organization, in 1820, attempted to exercise jurisdiction north of the Fulton line. The people refused to acquiesce, and the attempt was abandoned.

On the 22d of December, 1834, the General Assembly of Ohio adopted a memorial to Congress, in which this language occurs: "The occupation by the Territory of Michigan, of an integral part of her domain, has thus far been suffered by Ohio, because of its unimportance, while the northwestern quarter of the State remained a wilderness," etc.

This memorial was duly presented to Congress, and at the session of 1834-5, John Quincy Adams made an elaborate report against the claim of Ohio.

In the case of Daniels *vs.* Stevens' lessee, reported in the 19th Ohio Reports, Chief Justice Hitchcock, in delivering the opinion of the court, says: "At the session of the General Assembly at which this memorial was adopted, that body seems to have come to the determination to assert the rights of the State without further delay for the action of Congress. By an act passed Feb. 23d, 1835, (33 Ohio L. L. 92) entitled 'an act defining the northern boundary of certain counties in this State,' it is provided in the first section, 'that the counties of Williams, Henry, Wood,' etc., 'shall extend to, and be bounded on the north by a line run from the southern extremity of Lake Michigan to the most northern cape of Maumee Bay,' etc. The same act provides that certain townships north of the Fulton line shall be attached to the counties which they adjoin. All the provisions of this act, go to show that up to the time of its passage the jurisdiction over the territory had been in Michigan.

"By the same act the governor was authorized to appoint commissioners to survey the northern boundary of the State, according to the proviso in the constitution. Commissioners were appointed accordingly, but they were prevented from running this line by the people of Michigan. In consequence of this failure and the resistance of Michigan, the General Assembly was convened in special session on the 8th of June, 1835, at which session the county of Lucas was organized, made up, in a great measure, of this disputed territory. This, however, did not quiet the difficulty, for although the court of common pleas attempted to exercise, and did, to a certain extent, exercise jurisdiction, still, according to the agreed case, Michigan exercised the same jurisdiction as before. The difficulty was not ended until June, 1836, when Congress passed a law fixing this boundary in accordance with the wishes of Ohio."

Questions—By the ordinance of 1787 what was contemplated as to the dividing line between the tiers of States to be erected out of the Northwestern Territory? What action was taken by Congress on the 30th of April, 1802? What is said of the action of the constitutional convention? What action was taken by Congress in 1805? By the General Assembly of Ohio in 1807? By the Surveyor-General in 1812? What were the lines claimed by Ohio and Michigan called? What is said of the exercise of jurisdiction over the disputed territory prior to 1835? What action was taken by the General Assembly on the 22d of December, 1834? What was done with and in relation to this memorial? What were the provisions of the act of the General Assembly of date February 23d, 1835, entitled "an act defining the northern boundary of certain counties in this State"? What is said of the appointment of commissioners? Of the special session of the General Assembly? When was the dispute ended?

CHAPTER XI.

THE OHIO AND MICHIGAN, OR TOLEDO WAR, CONTINUED—SETTLEMENT OF THE DIFFICULTY BY CONGRESS.

At the spring election of 1836, a double set of local officers were elected in the townships embraced within the disputed territory, one set under Michigan laws and one under the laws of Ohio.

The sheriff of Monroe county, Michigan, at the head of a considerable force, marched into the disputed territory, and carried off to Monroe, some of the would-be citizens of Ohio, who aspired to the honor of the local officers under the laws of Ohio. Thereupon Gov. Lucas of Ohio levied troops and encamped at old Fort Miami, eight miles above Toledo, and four miles above the disputed territory.

Michigan was about to apply for admission as a State, and insisted on the line as originally established, and made preparations to resist a party of surveyors sent by the authorities of Ohio to re-survey the line. The surveyors were driven off by a party of Michigan men. Learning that Ohio would send troops to take possession of the disputed territory, acting Governor Mason called out the militia of the Territory, and as commander-in-chief, placed himself at their head, and marched "to the front."

No enemy appearing to oppose him, he marched boldly into Toledo, overrunning, it is said, all the watermelon patches in his route, and making sad havoc among the fowls of the neighboring farmers. "He demolished the ice-house of Maj. Stickney, burst in the front door of his residence, and triumphantly carried him off a prisoner of war to Monroe."

A case of considerable interest, Piatt *vs.* Oliver, in which the question of State jurisdiction became important, is reported in 2 *McLean*, 267, (U. S. Circuit Court) establishing the right of jurisdiction to be in Michigan until 1836. The case was appealed to the Supreme Court of the United States, where the jurisdiction over the disputed territory was treated as rightfully and clearly in Michigan. 3 *Howard's R.* 333.

The acts passed by the General Assembly of Ohio, in relation to the "Northern Boundary," indicated a determination to hold the disputed territory, if blood and treasure could do it. On the 19th of June, 1835, three hundred thousand dollars were appropriated, "to be paid out of the treasury on the order of the Auditor of State for the purpose of *defraying the expense of carrying into effect the laws* in regard to the northern boundary."

The following account of the conclusion of the war was furnished by an actor in the "scenes which he depicts," and published in Howe's Historical Collection:

"About this time appeared from the Court of Washington two ambassadors with full powers to negotiate with the belligerents for an amicable settlement of difficulties. These were Richard Rush, of Pennsylvania, and Colonel Howard, of Maryland. They were successful in their mission, chiefly because Michigan was satisfied with the laurels won, and Ohio was willing to stand on her dignity—eight miles from the ground in dispute. At the court next holden in Wood county, the prosecuting attorney presented bills of indictment against Gov. Mason and divers others in like manner offending; but the bills were thrown out by the grand jury. Thus was Ohio defeated in her resort to law, as she had before been in her passage at arms. At the next session of Congress the matter was taken up, and able arguments in favor of Ohio were made in the House, by Samuel F. Vinton, and in the Senate, by Thomas Ewing. Here, Ohio carried the day. Michigan, instead of the narrow strip averaging about eight miles wide on her southern border, received as an equivalent the large peninsula between Lakes Huron, Michigan, and Superior, now so well known for its rich deposits of copper and other minerals. The chief value to Ohio of the territory in dispute, was the harbor at Toledo, formed by the mouth of the Maumee, essential, as her public men believed, to enable her to reap the benefit of the commerce made by her canals to Cincinnati and Indiana. The result has shown that they judged correctly. Toledo has proved to be the true point for the meeting of lake and canal commerce."

Questions.—What is said of the spring election of 1836? What was done by the Sheriff of Monroe county? By Governor Lucas? What is said of the surveyors? Of Governor Mason? Which State did the courts decide had the rightful jurisdiction over the disputed territory? What appropriation was made by the General Assembly, and for what purpose? What is said of the negotiations for peace? Of certain indictments? How was the difficulty finally settled? In what way were both States benefitted by the final adjustment?

CHAPTER XII.*

OF THE PUBLIC LANDS—NAMES OF DIFFERENT TRACTS—CONGRESS LANDS, HOW SURVEYED—RESERVATION OF SEC. 16—THE SEVEN RANGES.

In most of the states and territories lying west of the Alleghany mountains, the United States, collectively, as a nation, owned, or did own, the soil of the country, after the extinguishment of the aboriginal Indian title.

When Ohio was admitted into the Federal Union as an independent State, one of the terms of admission was, that the fee-simple to all the lands within its limits, excepting those previously granted or sold, should vest in the United States. Different portions of them have, at different periods, been granted or sold to various individuals, companies and bodies politic.

The following are the names by which the principal bodies of the lands are designated, on account of these different forms of transfer, viz:

1. Congress Lands.	8. Symmes' Purchase.	15. Maumee Road Lands.
2. U. S. Military.	9. Refugee Tract.	16. School do.
3. Virginia Military.	10. French Grant.	17. College do.
4. Western Reserve.	11. Dohrman's do.	18. Ministerial do.
5. Fire Lands.	12. Zane's do.	19. Moravian do.
6. Ohio Co.'s Purchase.	13. Canal Lands.	20. Salt Sections.
7. Donation Tract.	14. Turnpike do.	

Congress Lands are so called because they are sold

*The matter composing this and the two following chapters was abridged from the Ohio Gazetteer, for Howe's Historical Collections, from which these chapters are copied.

to purchasers by the immediate officers of the general government, conformably to such laws as are, or may be, from time to time enacted by Congress. They are all regularly surveyed into townships of six miles square each, under authority, and at the expense of the national government.

All Congress lands, excepting Marietta and a part of Steubenville district, are numbered as follows:

6	5	4	3	2	1
7	8	9	10	11	12
18	17	16	15	14	13
19	20	21	22	23	24
30	29	28	27	26	25
31	32	33	34	35	36

VII ranges, Ohio Company's purchase, and Symmes' purchase are numbered as here exhibited:

36	30	24	18	12	6
35	29	23	17	11	5
34	28	22	16	10	4
33	27	21	15	9	3
32	26	20	14	8	2
31	25	19	13	7	1

The townships are again subdivided into sections of one mile square, each containing 640 acres, by lines running parallel with the township and range lines. The sections are numbered in two different modes, as exhibited in the preceding figures or diagrams.

In addition to the foregoing division, the sections are again subdivided into four equal parts, called the northeast quarter section, southeast quarter section, &c. And again, by a law of Congress which went into effect in July, 1820, these quarter sections are also divided by a north and south line into two equal parts, called the east half quarter section, No. —, and west half quarter section, No. —, which contain eighty acres each.

In establishing the township and sectional corners, a post is first planted at the intersection; then on the tree nearest the post, and standing within the section intended to be designated, is numbered with the marking-iron, the range, township, and number of the section, thus:

R 21	R 20
T 4	T 4
S 30	S 31
R 21	R 20
T 3	T 3
1	S 6

The quarter corners are marked "¼ south."

Section No. 16 of every township is perpetually reserved for the use of schools, and leased or sold out for the benefit of schools under the State Government. All the others may be taken up either in sections, fractions, halves, quarters, or half quarters.

For the purpose of selling out these lands they were divided into eight several land districts, called after the names of the towns in which the land offices were kept, viz: Wooster, Steubenville, Zanesville, Marietta, Chillicothe, etc., etc.

The seven ranges of townships are a portion of the Congress lands, so called, being the first ranges of public lands ever surveyed by the General Government west of of the Ohio river. They are bounded on the north by a line drawn due west from the Pennsylvania State line, where it crosses the Ohio river, to the United States military lands, 42 miles; thence south to the Ohio river, at the southeast corner of Marietta township, thence up the river to the place of beginning.

Questions.—What is said in this lesson as to the terms on which Ohio was admitted into the Union? By what names are the principal bodies of lands in this State designated? Why are *Congress Lands* so called? How are they surveyed? In what way are they numbered? How are these townships subdivided? The sections? How are sectional corners established and marked? What is said of section sixteen? Of land districts? Of the "Seven Ranges" of townships?

CHAPTER XIII.

OF THE PUBLIC LANDS, CONTINUED—THE CONNECTICUT WESTERN RESERVE, ITS HISTORY AND EXTENT—FIRE LANDS, ORIGIN OF NAME, HISTORY AND SURVEY OF—UNITED STATES MILITARY LANDS, THEIR HISTORY AND SURVEY—VIRGINIA MILITARY LANDS, HISTORY OF—OHIO COMPANY'S PURCHASE, EXTENT AND HISTORY OF.

Connecticut Western Reserve, oftentimes called New Connecticut, is situated in the northeast quarter of the State, between Lake Erie on the north, Pennsylvania east, the parallel of the 41st degree of north latitude south, and Sandusky and Seneca counties on the west. It extends 120 miles from east to west, and, upon an average, 50 miles from north to south; although upon the Pennsylvania line it is 68 miles broad, from north to south. The area is about 3,800,000 acres. It is surveyed into townships of five miles square, each. A body of half a million acres is, however, stricken off from the west end of the tract, as a donation, by the State of Connecticut, to certain sufferers by fire in the Revolutionary war.

The manner by which Connecticut became possessed

of the land question, was the following: King Charles II. of England, pursuing the example of his brother kings, of granting distant and foreign regions to his subjects, granted to the then colony of Connecticut, in 1662, a charter right to all lands included within certain specific bounds. But as the geographical knowledge of the Europeans concerning America was then very limited and confused, patents for lands often interfered with each other, and many of them, even by their express terms, extended to the Pacific ocean or South sea, as it was then called. Among the rest, that for Connecticut embraced all lands contained between the 41st and 42d parallels of north latitude, and from Providence plantations on the east to the Pacific ocean west, with the exception of New York and Pennsylvania colonies; and, indeed, pretensions to these were not finally relinquished without considerable altercation. And after the United States became an independent nation, these interfering claims occasioned much collision of sentiment between them and the State of Connecticut, which was finally compromised by the United States relinquishing all their claims upon, and guaranteeing to Connecticut the exclusive right of soil to the 3,800,000 acres already described. The United States, however, by the terms of compromise, reserved to themselves the right of jurisdiction. They then united this tract to the the Territory, now State of Ohio.

Fire Lands is a tract of country so called, of about 781 square miles, or 500,000 acres, in the western part of New Connecticut. The name originated from the circumstance of the State of Connecticut having granted these lands in 1792, as a donation to certain sufferers by fire, occasioned by the English during our Revolutionary war, particularly at New London, Fairfield and Norwalk. These lands include the five westernmost ranges of the Western Reserve townships. Lake Erie and Sandusky bay project so far southerly as to leave but the space of six tiers and some fractions of townships between them and the 41st parallel of latitude, or a tract of about of 30 by 27 miles in extent.

This tract is surveyed into townships of about five miles square each; and these townships are then subdivided into four quarters; and these quarter townships are numbered as in the accompanying figure, the top being considered north. And, for individual convenience, these are again subdivided by private surveys into lots of from fifty to five hundred acres each, to suit individual purchasers.

3	2
4	1

United States Military Lands are so called from the circumstance of their having been appropriated, by an act of Congress of the 1st of June, 1796, to satisfy certain claims of the officers and soldiers of the Revolutionary war. The tract of country embracing these lands is bounded as follows: Beginning at the northwest corner of the original VII ranges of townships, thence south 50 miles, thence west to the Scioto river, thence up said river to the Greenville treaty line, thence northeasterly with said line to old Fort Laurens, on the Tuscarawas river, thence due east to the place of beginning; including a tract of about 4,000 square miles, or 2,560,000 acres of land. It is, of course, bounded north by the Greenville treaty line, east by the VII ranges of townships, south by the Congress and Refugee lands, and west by the Scioto river.

These lands are surveyed into townships of five miles square. These townships were then again, originally, surveyed into quarter townships of two and a half miles square, containing 4,000 acres each; and subsequently, some of these quarter townships were subdivided into forty lots of 100 acres each, for the accommodation of those soldiers holding warrants for only one hundred acres each. And, again, after the time originally assigned for the location of these warrants had expired, certain quarter townships which had not then been located, were divided into sections of one mile square each, and sold by the General Government like the main body of Congress lands.

The quarter townships are numbered as exhibited in the accompanying figure, the top being considered north. The place of each township is ascertained by numbers and ranges, the same as Congress lands; the ranges being numbered from east to west, and the numbers from south to north.

2	1
3	4

Virginia Military Lands are a body of land lying between the Scioto and Little Miami rivers, and bounded by the Ohio river on the south. The State of Virgina, from the indefinite and vague terms of expression in its original colonial charter of territory from James I., King of England, in the year 1609, claimed all the Continent west of the Ohio river, and of the north and south breadth of Virginia. But finally, among several other compromises of conflicting claims which were made subsequently to the attainment of our national independence, Virginia agreed to relinquish all her claims to lands northwest of the Ohio river, in favor of the General Government, upon condition of the lands, now described, being guaranteed to her. The State of Virginia then appropriated this body of land to satisfy the claims of her State troops employed in the Continental line, during the Revolutionary war.

This district is not surveyed into townships or any regular form; but any individual holding a Viginia military land warrant may locate it wherever he chooses, within the district, and in such shape as he pleases, wherever the land shall not previously have been located. In consequence of this deficiency of regular original surveys, and the irregularities with which the several locations have been made, and the consequent interfence and encroachment of some locations upon others, more than double the litigation has probably arisen between the holders of adverse titles, in this district, than there has in any other part of the State, of equal extent.

Ohio Company's purchase is a body of land containing about 1,500,000 acres, including, however, the donation tract, school lands, &c., lying along the Ohio river, and including Meigs, nearly all of Athens, and a considerable part of Washington and Gallia counties. This tract was purchased of the General Government in the year 1787, by Manasseh Cutler and Winthrop Sargeant, from the neighborhood of Salem, in Massachusetts, agents for the "Ohio Company," which had then been formed in Massachusetts, for the purpose of a settlement in the Ohio country. Only 964,285 acres were ultimately paid for, and of course patented. This body of land was then apportioned into 817 shares, of 1173 acres each, and a town lot of one-third of an acre to each share. These shares were made up to each proprietor in tracts, one of 640 acres, one of 262, one of 160, one of 100, one of 8, and another of 3 acres, besides the before mentioned town lot.

Besides every section 16, set apart, as elsewhere, for the support of schools, every section 29 is appropriated for the support of religious institutions. In addition to which were also granted two townships six miles square for the use of a college.

But unfortunately for the Ohio Company, owing to their want of topographical knowledge of the country, the body of land selected by them, with some partial exceptions, is the most hilly and sterile of any tract of similar extent in the State.

Questions.—In what part of the State is the Western Reserve situated? What is its extent, and how many acres of land does it embrace? What is the size of the townships? In what manner did Connecticut become possessed of these lands? What is said in relation to these claims? Where are the so called "Fire Lands" located? Give the origin of the name. What do these lands include? How are they surveyed? Give the history of the U. S. Military Lands. Bound them. How many square miles or acres are embraced in this tract? How were these lands surveyed and numbered? Give the history of the Virginia Military Lands. What is said with reference to surveys? How many acres of land were embraced in the Ohio Company's purchase? What is said of this purchase? Of their apportionment? Of Sec. 16 and other lands?

CHAPTER XIV.

OF THE PUBLIC LANDS CONTINUED—DONATION TRACT—SYMMES' PURCHASE—REFUGEE TRACT—FRENCH GRANT—DOHRMAN'S GRANT — MORAVIAN LANDS—ZANE'S TRACTS — MAUMEE ROAD LANDS—TURNPIKE LANDS—CANAL LANDS—SCHOOL LANDS—COLLEGE TOWNSHIPS—MINISTERIAL LANDS—SALT SECTIONS.

Donation tract is a body of 100,000 acres, set off in the Ohio Company's tract, and granted to them by Congress, provided they should obtain one actual settler upon each hundred acres thereof, within five years from the date of the grant; and that so much of the 100,000 acres aforesaid, as should not thus be taken up, shall revert to the General Government.

This tract may, in some respects, be considered a part of the Ohio Company's purchase. It is situated in the northern limits of Washington county. It lies in an oblong shape, extending nearly 17 miles from east to west, and about 7½ from north to south.

Symmes' purchase is a tract of 311,682 acres of land, in the southwestern quarter of the State, between the Great and Little Miami rivers. It borders on the Ohio river a distance of 27 miles, and extends so far back from the latter between the two Miamis, as to include the quantity of land just mentioned. It was patented to John Cleves Symmes, in 1794, for 67 cents per acre. Every 16th section, or square mile, in each township, was reserved by Congress for the use of schools, and section 29 for the support of religious institutions, beside 15 acres around Fort Washington, in Cincinnati. This tract of country is now one of the most valuable in the State.

Refugee tract is a body of 100,000 acres of land granted by Congress to certain individuals who left the British provinces during the Revolutionary war, and espoused the cause of freedom. It is a narrow strip of country, 4½ miles broad from north to south, and extending eastwardly from the Scioto river 48 miles. It has the United States' XX ranges of Military or Army lands north, and XXII ranges of Congress lands south. In the western borders of this tract is situated the town of Columbus.

French grant is a tract of 24,000 acres of land, bordering upon the Ohio river, in the southeastern quarter of Scioto county. It was granted by Congress, in March, 1795, to a number of French families who lost their lands at Gallipolis, by invalid titles. Twelve hundred acres additional were afterwards granted, adjoining the above mentioned tract at its lower end, toward the mouth of Little Scioto river.

Dohrman's grant is one six mile square township, of 23,040 acres, granted to Arnold Henry Dohrman, formerly a wealthy Portuguese merchant in Lisbon, for and in consideration of his having, during the Revolutionary war, given shelter and aid to the American cruisers and vessels of war. It is located in the southeastern part of Tuscarawas county.

Moravian lands are three several tracts of 4,000 acres each, originally granted by the old Continental Congress,

July, 1787, and confirmed, by the act of Congress of 1st June, 1796, to the Moravian brethern at Bethlehem, in Pennsylvania, in trust for the use of the christianized Indians living thereon. They are laid out in nearly square forms, on the Muskingum river, in what is now Tuscarawas county. They are called by the names of the Shoenbrun, Gnadenhutten and Salem tracts.

Zane's tracts are three several tracts of one mile square each—one on the Muskingum, which includes the town of Zanesville—one at the cross of the Hocking river, on which the town of Lancaster is laid out—and the third on the left bank of the Scioto river, opposite Chillicothe. They were granted by Congress to one Ebenezer Zane, in May, 1796, on condition that he should open a road through them, from Wheeling, in Virginia, to Maysville, in Kentucky.

There are also three other tracts, of one mile square each, granted to Isaac Zane, in the year 1802, in consideration of his having been taken prisoner by the Indians, when a boy, during the Revolutionary war, and living with them most of his life, and having, during that time, performed many acts of kindness and beneficence toward the American people. These tracts are situated in Champain county, on King's creek, from three to five miles northwest from Urbana.

The Maumee road lands, are a body of lands, averaging two miles wide, lying along one mile on each side of the road from the Maumee river at Perrysburg, to the western limits of the Western Reserve, a distance of about 46 miles, and comprising nearly 60,000 acres. They were originally granted by the Indian owners, at the treaty of Brownstown in 1808, to enable the United States to make a road on the line just mentioned. The General Government never moved in the business, until February, 1823, when Congress passed an act, making over the aforesaid lands to the State of Ohio, provided she would, within four years thereafter, make and keep in repair, a good road throughout the aforesaid route of 46 miles. This road the State Government has already made; and obtained possession of, and sold most if not all of the land.

Turnpike lands are forty-nine sections, amounting to 31,360 acres, situated along the western side of the Columbus and Sandusky turnpike, in the eastern parts of Seneca, Crawford and Marion counties. They were originally granted by an act of Congress, on the 3d of March, 1827, and more specifically by a supplementary act, the year following. The considerations for which these lands were granted, were that the mail stages and all troops and property of the United States, which should ever be moved and transported along this road, shall pass free from toll.

The Ohio Canal Lands are lands granted by Congress to the State of Ohio to aid in constructing her extensive canals. These lands comprise over one million of acres.

School lands. By compact between the United States and the State of Ohio, when the latter was admitted into the Union, it was stipulated, for and in consideration that the State of Ohio should never tax the Congress lands, until after they should have been sold five years, and in consideration that the public lands would thereby more readily sell, that the one thirty-sixth part of all the territory included within the limits of the State, should be set apart for the support of common schools therein. And for the purpose of getting at lands which should, in point of quality of soil be on an average with the whole land in the country, they agreed that it should be selected by lot in small tracts each, to wit: that it should consist of section number 16, let that section be good or bad, in every township of Congress lands; also in the Ohio Company's, and in Symmes' purchases; all of which townships are composed of 36 sections each; and for the United States' military lands, and Connecticut Reserve, a number of quarter townships, 2½ miles square each, (being the smallest public surveys therein, then made,) should be selected by the Secretary of the Treasury, in different places throughout the United States' military tract, equivalent in quantity, to the one thirty-sixth part of those two tracts respectively. And for the Virginia military tract, Congress enacted that a quantity of land equal to the one thirty-sixth part of the estimated quantity of land contained therein, should be selected by lot, in what was then called the "New Purchase," in quarter township tracts of three miles square each. Most of these selections were accordingly made; but in some instances by the carelessness of the officers conducting the sales, or from some other cause, a few sections 16 have been sold; in which case, Congress, when applied to, has generally granted other lands in lieu thereof; as for instance, no section 16 was reserved in Montgomery township, in which Columbus is situated; and Congress, afterwards granted therefor, section 21, in the township cornering thereon to the south-east.

College townships are three six miles square townships, granted by Congress; two of them to the Ohio Company, for the use of a college to be established within their purchase, and one for the use of the inhabitants of Symmes' purchase.

Ministerial Lands. In both the Ohio Company's and in Symmes' purchase, every section 29, (equal to one thirty-sixth part of every township,) is reserved, as a permanent fund for the support of a settled minister. As the purchasers of these two tracts came from parts of the Union where it was customary and deemed necessary to have a regular settled clergyman in every town, they therefore stipulated in their original purchase, that a permanent fund, in land, should thus be set apart for this purchase. In no other part of the State, other than in these two purchases, are any lands set apart for this object.

Salt Sections. Near the centre of what is now Jackson county, Congress originally reserved from sale thirty-six sections, or one six mile square township, around and including what was called the Scioto salt licks; also one quarter of a five mile square township in what is now Delaware county; in all, forty-two and a quarter sections, or 27,040 acres. By an act of Congress of the 28th of December, 1824, the Legislature of Ohio was authorized to sell these lands, and to apply the proceeds thereof to such literary purposes as said Legislature may think proper but to no other purpose whatever.

Questions—Give the history and extent of the Donation tract. Of the Symmes' purchase. What reservations did the Government make? Give the history and extent of the Refugee tract. Of the French grant. Of Dohrman's grant. Of the Moravian lands. Of Zane's tracts. Of the Maumee road lands. Of the Turnpike lands. Of the Canal lands. Of School lands. Of College townships. Of Ministerial lands. Of Salt sections.

CHAPTER XV.

THE VALLEYS OF OHIO.

It is quite common in referring to different sections of the State to designate them as "Valleys."

For the purpose of considering the capabilities of different localities, with reference to agriculture, the Hon. John H. Klippart, secretary of the state board of agriculture, has divided the State into districts, designating them and defining their limits as follows:

I. *Miami Valley*, consisting of the counties of Butler, Brown, Champaign, Clarke, Clermont, Clinton, Darke, Green, Hamilton, Logan, Miami, Montgomery, Preble, and Shelby.

II. *Maumee Valley*, consisting of Allen, Auglaize, Crawford, Defiance, Fulton, Hancock, Henry, Lucas, Mercer, Ottowa, Paulding, Putnam, Sandusky, Seneca, Van Wert, Williams, Wood, and Wyandot counties.

III. *Scioto Valley*, consisting of Adams, Delaware, Fayette, Franklin, Hardin, Highland, Jackson, Madison, Marion, Morrow, Pickaway, Pike, Ross, Scioto, and Union counties.

IV. *Muskingum Valley*, consisting of Ashland, Carroll, Coshocton, Guernsey, Harrison, Holmes, Knox, Licking, Muskingum, Morgan, Noble, Richland, Stark, Tuscarawas, Washington, and Wayne counties.

V. *Western Reserve*, consisting of Ashtabula, Cuyahoga, Erie, Geauga, Huron, Lake, Lorain, Mahoning, Medina, Portage, Summit, and Trumbull counties.

VI. *Hocking Valley*, consisting of Athens, Fairfield, Gallia, Hocking, Lawrence, Meigs, Perry, and Vinton counties.

VII. The river counties, not belonging to any river system other than the Ohio, are Belmont, Columbiana, Jefferson and Monroe.

Questions—Name the seven districts of the State as designated by the secretary of the state board of agriculture. What counties are embraced within the Miami Valley? The Maumee Valley? The Scioto Valley? The Muskingum Valley? The Western Reserve? The Hocking Valley? The River counties?

CHAPTER XVI.

THE COAL FIELDS OF OHIO—IRON ORE.

The counties wholly covered with coal are Mahoning, Columbiana, Stark, Holmes, Tuscarawas, Carroll, Jefferson, Harrison, Belmont, Guernsey, Coshocton, Muskingum, Perry, Noble, Morgan, Monroe, Washington, Athens, Meigs, Gallia, Lawrence, and nearly all of Jackson. All the counties of which the eastern or southeastern parts only are covered with coal, are Trumbull, Portage, Summit, Medina, Wayne, Licking, Fairfield, Hocking, Vinton, andScioto. There are also some outliers or small detached basins in Wayne, Ashland, Richland, and Knox counties.

The boundary on the east is the State line, the same field extending eastward over all western Pennsylvania.*

Outline Map of the Geological Formations of Ohio.

The coals of Ohio belong to the great Alleghany coal field, which extends from northern Pennsylvania to central Alabama, a distance of over 700 miles. This coal ba-

*Macfarlane's Coal Regions of America.

sin of irregular breadth, has an area of about 63,822 square miles, of which Ohio has more than than 10,000, or about 6,500,000 acres.

The coal area of Ohio alone equals that of Great Britain, and is six times greater than that of France, Prussia, or Austria, and about four times greater than that of Spain, which has a greater extent of coal territory than any other nation on the continent. Great Britain owes her greatness as a commercial and manufacturing nation to this sure source of wealth and power, though her mines are many hundred feet deep, and are worked with great labor and risk of life.

The average aggregate thickness of the available seams is 20 feet. (The State geologists say this is a low estimate). There are 27 cubic feet to the ton. This gives 209,733,333,340 tons for the State. At the rate the mines of the State now yield, this amount would not be exhausted in 51,200 years, or would stand the present draft on all the mines of the United States for 4,560 years; or with a yearly product equal to that of the mines of Great Britain, it would last 1,600 years.

Ohio coals are all bituminous, and are divided by our State geologists into three classes: first, furnace coal; second, coking coal; third, cannel coal. The first variety has the largest per cent. of fixed carbon, and is best adapted to the manufacture of iron from ore, being used for this purpose in the raw state. Half the iron made in the State is made from this variety. Several coal seams extending over large sections, including the great seam in Athens and Perry counties, also the lowest stratum, which, at the places of its northern outcrop, is called Brier Hill coal, are of this valuable open burning variety.

The second class requires coking before using in the blast furnace, because of its tendency to cement when heated. It has a resinous luster, and breaks into trapezoidal blocks.

Cannel coal is very compact, forms an excellent fuel for ordinary purposes, and yields a large quantity of superior illuminating gas. It resembles a dark shale, and contains a large quantityof bitumen.*

In Ohio are found in proximity, and in quantities almost inexhaustible, iron ore, coal and limestone—the materials necessary for the manufacture of pig iron—with a good home market, and river, lake, canal, and railroad transportation to markets outside the State. Her superior natural advantages will enable Ohio to maintain her present rank as second of the iron manufacturing States.

The mining of iron ore in the State has been confined chiefly to the counties of Carroll, Columbiana, Fairfield, Hocking, Jackson, Lawrence, Muskingum, Perry, Scioto, Stark, Trumbull, Tuscarawas, Vinton, and Washington.

Questions—Name the counties wholly covered with coal. Name those partially covered. To what great field do the coals of Ohio belong? What is the extent of this field? The extent of the coal basin of Ohio? Average thickness of the coal seams of Ohio? How many cubic feet of coal are there to the ton? How many tons would this estimate give to the State? How long would it take to exhaust the mines of the State, at the rate of their present yield? How long, if they yielded annually as much as all the mines of the United States now yield? How long, if its annual yield was equal to that of the mines of Great Britain? Into what classes do our State geologists divide Ohio coals? Give the peculiarities and use of each class? What is said of iron ore? To what counties has the mining of iron ore thus far been confined?

---

*Report of Hon. Allen T. Wikoff, Secretary of State.

CHAPTER XVII.

AGRICULTURAL STATISTICS—FRUIT CROPS—LIVE STOCK.

The statistics for 1870 show the following in regard to the lands of Ohio: Acres of cultivated land, 15,444,-691; acres of uncultivated or wood land 9,815,382; total amount in farms, 25,260,073; number of farms, 195,953; average number of acres of improved land in each farm, 78.8.

Of the different varieties of timber with which the State abounds, are black walnut, oak, hickory, poplar, maple, beach, ash, cherry, and whitewood.

The following table, compiled from the assessors' returns for 1872, will show the agricultural products of the State. The wheat crop of 1874 was unusually large. The returns for 1872 will give about the average yield per annum for a series of years:

Crops.	Acres.	Bushels.
Corn,	2,520,253	103,053,234
Oats,	971,494	25,825,742
Wheat,	1,611,217	18,087,664
Barley,	72,483	1,528,266
Rye,	25,166	295,843
Buckwheat,	34,882	266,807
Total	5,235,495	149,057,556

Dividing the State into three districts, the northern, middle and southern, for the purpose of comparing them as wheat-growing regions, and we have the following result:

NORTHERN DISTRICT.—Thirty-three counties; average per acre, in 1872, 14.66 bushels.

CENTRAL DISTRICT.—Thirty-three counties; average per acre, in 1872, 9.94 bushels.

SOUTHERN DISTRICT.—Twenty-two counties; average per acre, in 1872, 8.72 bushels.

The following table shows the average number of bushels of corn per acre in the districts below mentioned, respectively, in the years 1868, 1869, 1870, 1871 and 1872:

DISTRICT.	Bushels per acre, 1868.	Bushels per acre, 1869.	Bushels per acre, 1870.	Bushels per acre, 1871.	Bushels per acre, 1872.
Miami Valley	38.12	30.07	38.92	40.43	41.82
Western Reserve	37.89	32.24	44.60	43.75	47.41
Hocking Valley	34.98	29.96	30.04	31.75	35.65
Scioto Valley	34.62	27.86	36.16	33.39	40.97
Muskingum Valley	33.69	38.88	37.59	38.68	42.59
Maumee Valley	32.22	17.58	39.65	39.68	39.74
Ohio River counties	29.98	29.25	33.16	37.04	35.15

The production of potatoes in the State in 1872 was as follows:

Acres planted	105,896
Bushels produced	7,832,297
Average yield per acre	73.96

The sweet-potato crop in 1872 was as follows:

Acres planted	3,026
Bushels produced	215,023
Average yield per acre	71.

The crop of timothy hay in the State in 1872 was as follows:

Acres in meadow 1,322,387
Tons of hay produced 1,270,779
Average number of tons per acre .... .96, or 24-25 of a ton.

The products of the dairy in Ohio in 1872 were as follows:

Pounds of butter 45,413,066
Pounds of cheese 34,403,857

The Western Reserve is the great dairy region of the State, about sixteen-seventeenths of all the cheese of the State being made in that district:

The acres in orchards and their products for the five years preceding and including 1872, were reported as follows:

YEARS.	Acres.	Bushels apples.	Bushels peaches.	Bushels pears.
1868	342,212	11,637,515	599,499	66,712
1869	346,826	15,518,685	1,444,523	147,022
1870	377,297	11,012,582	309,639	67,047
1871	383,647	10,437,437	860,530	126,982
1872	391,550	21,632,475	405,619	153,968

The climate of Ohio is favorable for grape culture. The crop in the entire State ranges from ten to twenty million pounds per annum. The four counties producing the largest amount are Ottawa, Erie, Cuyahoga and Lorain.

Number and value of horses, cattle and mules in Ohio, in 1874:

HORSES.		CATTLE.		MULES, ETC.	
Number.	Value.	Number.	Value.	Number.	Value.
729,303	$46,137,368	1,673,864	$27,917,537	25,345	$1,777.181

Number and value of sheep and hogs in Ohio in 1874:

SHEEP.	Number,--4,333,868 Value, --$10,452,067	HOGS.	Number, -------1,915,220 Value,---------$6,152,875

The total value of property, as returned to the Auditor of State, for 1874, is as follows:

Real estate in cities, towns, and villages	$354,849,199 00
Real estate not in cities, towns, or villages	697,408,537 00
Chattel property	528,121,588 00
Total taxable values for 1874	$1,580,379,324 00

Questions—How many acres of cultivated lands, as shown by the returns of 1870, were there in Ohio? Uncultivated? In farms? Give the number of farms. Average number of acres of improved land to each farm. Mention the leading varieties of timber. Give the number of acres in corn, and the number of bushels raised in the State in 1872. Of oats. Of wheat. Of barley. Of rye. Of buckwheat. What was the average, per acre, of wheat in 1872, in the northern 33 counties? In the middle 33 counties? In the southern 22 counties? From the table given, name the seven districts in order, with reference to their productiveness as corn growing regions, commencing with the district producing the most per acre, for the five years given. What was the yield per acre of potatoes in 1872? Of sweet potatoes? Of hay? How many pounds of butter were manufactured? Of cheese? What is said of the Western Reserve as a dairy region? How many acres were in orchard in 1872? What is said of grape culture? Give the number and value of horses, cattle, and mules in the State in 1874? Of sheep and hogs? What was the total valuation of taxable property in the State in 1874?

CHAPTER XVIII.

OHIO CANALS*.

There are 658 miles of canals proper, 91 miles of the Muskingum slack-water improvement, 36 miles of feeders and side-cuts, and 11 miles of reservoirs in Ohio, making a total of 796 miles, all navigable, with 306 lift and 10 guard locks. The first canal was commenced in 1825, and the last one completed in 1842. Total cost, $14,688,666.97, being an average cost per mile of $18,453.09.

Ohio Canal—Cleveland to Portsmouth. The main line was commenced in 1825, and completed in 1833. The total length of main lines, feeders and side-cuts is 331 miles. Total cost, $4,695,203 69.

Miami and Erie Canal—Cincinnati to Manhatten. This canal was commenced in 1826 and completed from Cincinnati to Dayton in 1833; from Dayton to Junction, 1844; from Junction to Manhatten, 1838–1842; from Junction to State line, 1838–1842. The total length of main line, feeders and reservoirs, is 293 miles. The cost of construction was $7,463,694 99.

That portion of the main line (4 miles) between Manhatten and Toledo, has been abandoned.

Walhonding Canal—Roscoe to Rochester. The main line was let in 1836 and completed in 1842. Its length is 25 miles. The cost of construction was $607,-268 99.

*From the official report of Hon. Allen T. Wikoff, Secretary of State.

Hocking Canal—Carroll to Athens. The main line was commenced in 1836, and finished in 1842. Its length is 56 miles. The cost of construction was $975,481.01.

Muskingum Improvement—Dresden to Marietta. The length of improvement, commenced in 1836 and finished in 1842, is 91 miles. The cost of the improvement, including locks and dams, was $1,627,018 29.

Warren County Canal—This work cost the State $217,552 16. It was long ago abandoned by act of the General Assembly. It was intended to be a branch of the Miami Canal, from Franklin to Lebanon, in Warren county.

Questions—How many miles of canals are there in the State? Of the Muskingum slackwater improvement? Of feeders and side-cuts? Of reservoirs? How many lift locks? Guard locks? What is said in this lesson of the Ohio canal? Miami and Erie? Walhonding? Hocking? Muskingum improvement? Warren county canal?

CHAPTER XIX.

THE RAILROADS OF OHIO.

The present (1875) aggregate length of railroads in the State, including main lines, branches, sidings, and other tracks is about 5,500 miles.

The average cost of these roads, per mile, including equipment, is $54,465.

In 1825, the Liverpool and Manchester Railroad, in

England, was opened, and the cars were drawn by a locomotive. It is said that this was the first real success of the locomotive.

The experience of the English roads stimulated the active minds of America, and in 1830 measures were ~~inaugurated for the introduction of~~ steam cars in this country.

The legislative records of this State show that in 1831, 1832, 1833, 1835, and 1836, many railroad charters were granted. While some of the roads then contemplated have never been built, most of them have been.

The Cincinnati, Sandusky and Cleveland Railroad was chartered June 5th, 1832; the Little Miami Railroad Company, March 11, 1836; Cleveland, Columbus and Cincinnati, March 14, 1836; Sandusky, Mansfield and Newark, March 9, 1835.

"It is said that the first actual piece of railroad was made on the Cincinnati and Sandusky road; but about the same time was made the Little Miami road, and of that we have a record. The Little Miami Railroad was first surveyed in 1836-37.

"The Little Miami road was commenced about 1840, and a considerable part had been made in 1842, and its first annual report made in that year. In 1849 the road was in operation to Xenia, and in 1851-2 the Xenia and Columbus road was made. In 1852, according to Andrews' report on American trade, there were in Ohio (in whole or in part) thirteen lines of railroad, making in all 1,154 miles *in operation*."*

*From Review of the History, &c., of Railroads in Ohio, by E. D. Mansfield, LL. D.

From 1852 to the present time, more than 4,000 miles of railroad have been built in Ohio.

It is impossible to state with certainty all the advantages derived from our system of railroads, though we might give some practical illustrations, if space would permit. The following, however, must suffice:

"In 1825–6, when the Ohio canal had been begun, wheat sold at Massillon (in the wheat section of the State) at 37½ cents per bushel. On the completion of the canal, an average of 50 cents per bushel was added and in the last fifteen years, an average of 50 cents more by the railroads. Ohio averages an exportation of 12,000,000 bushels of wheat per annum, so that the *gain* to farmers on the single item of wheat was $6,000,000 per annum. But the gain in *interest* by the saving of *time* was nearly as great."*

Questions—What is the aggregate length of railroads in Ohio? Average cost per mile? When and where was the succcess of the railroad locomotive first demonstrated? When were measures inaugurated for the introduction of steam cars in America? What is said of railroad charters in Ohio? Give the names of some of the earliest railroad corporations in Ohio, and the date of their charters. What is said of the construction of the first railroads in the State? What illustration is given to show the value of canals and railroads?

---

*From the Review of the History, &c., of Railroads in Ohio, by E. P. Mansfield, L. L. D.

CHAPTER XX.

GOVERNORS OF OHIO.

Arthur St. Clair, of Pennsylvania, was governor of the Northwest Territory, of which Ohio was a part, from July 13, 1788, when the first civil government was established in the Territory, until about the close of the year 1802, when he was removed by the President.

Charles W. Bird was secretary of the Territory at the time of the removal of Governor St. Clair, and thereupon became acting governor.

Edward Tiffin was the first governor after the organization of the State government. His term commenced March 3d, 1803. Resigned March 3d, 1807, to accept the office of United States Senator.

Thomas Kirker, speaker of the State Senate, by virtue of his office succeeded Governor Tiffin for the balance of the unexpired term.

Return Jonathan Meigs was elected governor on the second Tuesday of Ooctober, 1807, over Nathaniel Massie, who contested the election of Meigs on the ground "that he had not been a resident of this State for four years next preceding the election, as required by the constitution," and the General Assembly, in joint convention, decided that he was not eligible. The office was not given to Massie, nor does it appear, from the records, that he claimed it, but Thomas Kirker, acting governor, continued to discharge the duties of the office until

Samuel Huntington was inaugurated, December 12, 1808, he having been elected on the second Tuesday of October, in that year.

Return Jonathan Meigs was re-elected in 1810, and entered upon the discharge of his official duties December 8, 1810. Resigned March 25, 1814, to accept the office of Postmaster General of the United States.

Othniel Looker, acting governor, succeeded to office, April 14, 1814, by reason of being speaker of the Senate.

Thomas Worthington was governor from December 8th, 1814, to Dec. 14, 1818.

Ethan Allen Brown was inaugurated December 14, 1818. Resigned January 4, 1822, to accept the office of United States Senator.

Allen Trimble, acting governor, succeeded to office January 7th, 1822, by reason of being speaker of the Senate.

Jeremiah Morrow, from Dec. 28, 1822, to Dec. 19, 1826.

Allen Trimble, from Dec. 19, 1826, to Dec. 18, 1830.

Duncan McArthur, from Dec. 18, 1830, to Dec. 7, 1832.

Robert Lucas, from Dec. 7, 1832, to Dec. 13, 1836.

Joseph Vance, from Dec. 13, 1836, to Dec. 13, 1838.

Wilson Shannon, from Dec. 13, 1838, to Dec. 16, 1840.

Thomas Corwin, from Dec. 16, 1840, to Dec. 14, 1842.

Wilson Shannon, inaugurated Dec. 13, 1838. Resigned April 13, 1844, to accept the office of minister to Mexico.

Thomas W. Bartley, acting governor, succeeded to office, April 13, 1844, by reason of being speaker of the Senate.

Mordecai Bartley, inaugurated Dec. 3, 1844. Term expired Dec. 12, 1846.

William Bibb, from Dec. 12, 1846, to January 22, 1849.

Seabury Ford was duly elected in 1848, but the result of the election in 1848 was not finally determined in joint convention of the two houses of the General Assembly until January 19, 1849, and the inauguration did not take place until the 22d of that month. Term expired Dec. 12, 1850.

Reuben Wood, inaugurated Dec. 12, 1850. Resigned July 15, 1853, to accept the office of consul to Valparaiso.

William Medill, acting governor, succeeded to office by reason of being lieutenant-governor, July 15, 1853. Elected in October, 1853, for the regular term, to commence on the second Monday of January, 1854. Term expired January 14, 1856.

Salmon P. Chase, from Jan. 14, 1856, to Jan. 9, 1860.

William Dennison, from Jan. 9, 1860, to January 13, 1862.

David Tod, from Jan. 13, 1862, to Jan. 12, 1864.

John Brough, inaugurated, Jan. 12, 1864. Died August 29, 1865.

Charles Anderson, acting governor, succeeded to office, by reason of being lieutenant-governor, August 30, 1865. Term expired Jan. 9, 1866.

Jacob D. Cox, from Jan. 9, 1866, to Jan. 13, 1868.

Rutherford B. Hayes, from Jan 13, 1868, to Jan. 8, 1872.

Edward F. Noyes, from Jan. 8, 1872, to Jan. 12, 1874.

William Allen, inaugurated Jan. 12, 1874.

Questions—Who was the first governor of the Northwest Territory as organized by the ordinance of 1787? When was he removed from office? Who was his successor? Who was the first governor after the State was organized? When and for what purpose did he resign? Who succeeded Governor Tiffin? What is said of the election of Return J. Meigs in 1807? Who succeeded Gov. Kirker? Who was elected in 1810? When and for what purpose did Governor Meigs resign? Name the persons who held the office of governor from 1814 to 1830. From 1830 to 1844. When and for what purpose did Governor Shannon resign? What persons held the office of governor from 1844 to 1848. What is said with reference to the election of Governor Ford? Who succeeded Governor Ford? When and for what purpose did Governor Wood resign? Name the persons who held the office of governor from 1853 to Aug. 29, 1865. From 1865 to 1875.

CHAPTER XXI.

OHIO IN THE WAR OF THE REBELLION.*

In the late war of the Rebellion, Ohio achieved for herself a glorious record. The following table will show the number of enlistments under the different calls of the President:

" Under the call of			No. furnished	Quota.
April 15, 1861	for	75,000 men	12,357	10,153†
July 22, 1861	"	500,000 "	84,116	67,365
July 2, 1862	"	300,000 "	58,325	36,858
August 4, 1862	"	300,000 " (for 9 months)	——	36,858
June 15, 1863	"	militia	2,736	——
October 17, 1863	"	500,000 "	32,837	51,465
March 14, 1864	"	200,000 "	29,931	20,595
April 22, 1864	"	one hundred days militia	36,254	30,000
July 18, 1864	"	500,000 men	30,823	27,001
December 19, 1864	"	300,000 "	23,275	26,027
Totals			310,654	306,322 "

In addition to this there were several thousand negro soldiers from Ohio, either credited to other States or to the "United States colored troops"; and over two thousand white men enlisted in the gun-boat service, for which the State had no credit.

Of this vast army furnished by the State, only 8,750 were raised by draft, the rest being volunteers.

*This chapter is compiled from a work entitled "Ohio in the War," by Whitelaw Reid.

†No credit was here given for the extra ten regiments raised for three months service in April and May, 1861, which the Government refused to accept.

The amount paid to volunteers in local bounties, was a little more than $23,500,000.

The military organizations of Ohio, in the field during the war, were 197 regiments of infantry, 13 regiments of cavalry, 13 batteries of light artillery, 2 regiments of heavy artillery, and 26 independent batteries. In addition to these there were 23 three-months organizations of which no systematic record was kept in the State Adjutant General's office.

"Their service was deadly. Eleven thousand two hundred and thirty-seven of them were killed or mortally wounded in action, of whom six thousand five hundred and sixty-three were left dead on the field of battle. Thirteen thousand three hundred and fifty four died, before the expiration of their terms of enlistment, of diseases contracted in the service. Thirty-seven Ohio soldiers out of every thousand, fell dead, mortally wounded in battle; forty-seven more died in the hospitals; seventy-one more were honorably discharged, unable longer to do the duty of soldiers, by reason of wounds or sickness incurred in the country's service. Let us not, in the fullness of our pride, conceal the darker side of the picture: forty-four out of every thousand deserted. But many of the desertions were not such in intention. After a stolen visit to their families the men went back to the service."

Questions—How many different calls were made upon Ohio for soldiers by the President, during the late war? What was the whole number required of the State? How many were furnished? How many were raised by draft? What amount was paid to volunteers in local bounties? How many regiments of infantry were furnished by the State? Of cavalry? Batteries of light artillery? Heavy artillery? Independent batteries? What is said of other organizations? How many Ohio soldiers were killed or mortally wounded in battle? How many were left dead on the field? How many died of disease? What proportion were killed or mortally wounded in battle? What proportion died in the hospitals? What proportion were discharged on account of wounds or sickness? What proportion deserted?

GOVERNMENT AND LAW.

CHAPTER XXII.

OF THE ORGANIZATION OF GOVERNMENT, AND THE EXERCISE OF SOVEREIGNTY.

~~To enable the people~~ to defend their rights and to do ~~right and~~ justice, ~~they~~ unite together in a body politic; and when ~~the people~~ are so united and have agreed upon certain rules by which they are to be governed, we speak of such union, in its most enlarged sense, as a State. Bouvier defines a State as follows: "In its most enlarged sense, it signifies a self-sufficient body of persons united together in one community for the defense of their rights and to do right and justice to foreigners."

In ~~a more limited~~ sense, a State means the territory occupied by the united body of people, as, the State of Ohio.

In many countries, the rulers are sovereign; that is, exercise control, authority and power as they see fit, regardless of the wishes or consent of the governed. But in this country no single individual has the right to exercise this power. Here the people choose their rulers, and, by written constitutions, define and limit their powers and duties.

Sovereignty, the supreme or highest power among men, in this country, resides in the people. This power, however, the people authorize their officers to exercise and, having instituted a government, they have agreed to submit to and abide by certain rules and regulations; have conferred power upon their officers to enforce obedience to such rules and regulations.

Government is defined as, "the manner in which sovereignty is exercised in each State."

In every State there is either some individual or body of men whose duty it is to see to the enforcement of the laws; and we sometimes refer to them as the Government.

Questions—What is a State, and for what purpose is it organized? Give Bouvier's definition of a State? What is a sovereign? With whom does sovereign power reside in this country? Who exercise the power of sovereignty in this country? In what way and by what authority are the people required to submit to the power we call sovereignty? What is government? In what other sense do we sometimes use the word government?

CHAPTER XXIII.

OF LAWS AND THEIR NECESSITY—RIGHTS AND DUTIES.

The rules of action adopted for the government of the people are called laws. Hence a law is that which commands us what to do and forbids the things we are not to do.

The necessity for these rules or laws is apparent when we observe and consider the many differences and difficulties among men which arise either from mistakes, honest disagreements, want of judgment, or intentional misconduct or wrong. They are necessary, to indicate to us our duties as members of society, and to protect us in the enjoyment of our rights.

A right is a legal title or a just claim to anything. We have a right to life, a right to our earnings, and a right to act as we please and to go where we please, provided we do not interfere with the rights of others.

These rights, however, are subject to certain restrictions or limitations and may be forfeited, or, when the public good requires it, may be taken from us. By violating the law we may forfeit our liberty and our property. If called upon to take up arms in behalf of the country, it is our duty to respond, and if needs be, to surrender our property and our lives.

As children are dependent upon their parents, they owe them certain duties, not the least of which is obedience to their commands. So with the citizen, dependent upon the State for the protection of himself and his property, he is bound to observe the rules prescribed for his conduct.

Questions.—What are human laws? How is the necessity for law apparent? For what are laws necessary? What is a right? Mention some of our rights. To what are these rights subject? How may we forfeit our liberty and property? What duty do we owe the country? State one of the grounds on which obedience is a duty.

CHAPTER XXIV.

OF THE DIFFERENT FORMS OF GOVERNMENT—CONSTITUTIONS, AND THE PURPOSE THEY SERVE.

Different forms of government prevail in different countries.

In those countries where the power to govern and make laws is vested in one person, we call the government a monarchy.

Where the great body of freemen assemble together to make the laws and transact the business of the State, we call the government a democracy.

Where the chief magistrate gets his power to rule by inheritance, but has no power to make the laws, we call the government a mixed government, or a limited monarchy. Such is the government of Great Britain. The laws are framed by Parliament, and when approved by the monarch become operative.

Where the people enjoy common rights and privileges, but exercise the sovereign power by and through representatives elected by them, we call the government a republic. Every State in the American Union is a republic.

A pure democracy and our American Republic differ in this, that in the former, the citizens assemble in a body to make the laws, while in the latter the people choose representatives to act for them. Both are governments of the people and derive their powers from them.

The form of government in each of the United States is represented by a written constitution. These constitutions are called the fundamental or political law. They are adopted as the agreement of the people—as the framework of the government—and limit the power of the various departments.

Any act of the General Assembly or of any officer of the State which conflicts with any of the provisions of the constitution is invalid. Thus the people are protected against unjust enactments and usurpation of power by their public servants.

Questions—Are the forms of government the same in all countries? What is a monarchy? What is a democracy? What is a mixed government or limited monarchy? What form of government has Great Britain? What is a republic? What form of government have the States of the American Union? Wherein consists the difference between a democracy and a republic? From whence do republics and democracies derive their power? By what are the forms of government represented in the several States of this Union? By what names are constitutions sometimes called? What is the object or purpose of constitutions? How do they protect the people?

CHAPTER XXV.

GOVERNMENT OF OHIO—DIVISIONS OF THE POWERS OF GOVERNMENT.

The powers of government are divided into three departments: the legislative, executive and judicial.

The legislative department is that which enacts the

laws for the government of the people, and its power is vested in a senate and house of representatives. These two houses constitute the General Assembly.

By the constitution the executive department consists of a Governor, Lieutenant-governor, Secretary of State, Auditor, Treasurer, and an Attorney-general. It is the duty of the executive department to see to it that the laws are carried into effect.

The constitution provides that the judicial power shall be vested in a Supreme Court, in district courts, courts of common pleas, courts of probate, justices of the peace and such other courts, inferior to the supreme court, in one or more counties, as the General Assembly may, from time to time, establish. It is the duty of this department to administer justice according to the laws. These duties will be considered more in detail, in subsequent chapters.

Questions—Into how many departments are the powers of government divided? Name them. What is the legislative department? What do the two houses of the legislature constitute? Of what officers does the executive department consist? What is the special duty of the executive department? In what courts is the judicial power vested? What is said of the duty of this department?

CHAPTER XXVI.

QUALIFICATIONS OF ELECTORS—NATURALIZATION OF FOREIGNERS.

The right to vote is called the right of suffrage.

Persons who have the right ~~to make choice of public officers, and~~ to vote, are called electors.

Every male citizen of the United States, except idiots or insane persons, of the age of twenty-one years, who shall have been a resident of the State one year next preceding the election, and the county, township or ward, in which he resides, such time as is provided by law, shall have the qualifications of an elector.

By law, persons to become electors, must have resided in the State for one year next preceding the election, and in the county for thirty days next preceding the election, and in the township, incorporated village or ward of a city or village for twenty days next preceding the election, at which such person shall offer to vote. But a voter, being the head of a family who removes from one part of the county to another is not required to reside at his new home, ~~to entitle him to vote,~~ for any particular length of time, except that he cannot vote at city or village elections unless he shall have resided ~~therein~~ twenty days prior to such election.

Persons born in other countries are called *aliens;* and to become citizens must be naturalized. To accomplish this, the person desiring to become a citizen must go before the court or the clerk thereof, two years before he can be admitted as a citizen, and declare on oath, in writing, that he intends to become a citizen of the United States, and to *renounce* his *allegiance* to his former government; and he must declare on oath that he will support the constitution of the United States. Then, two years thereafter, the court, if satisfied as to his *moral character* and loyalty, and that he has resided in the United States for five years, and in the State or Territory where the court is held, for one year, may admit him as a citizen.

Persons residing within and under the jurisdiction of the United States, at any time between the 18th of June, 1778, and April 14th, 1802, and who have continued to reside therein, are exempt from the provisions of the preceding paragraph.

Any alien being a minor, who arrives in the United States when not over eighteen years of age, and continues to reside therein, may, after he arrives at the age of twenty-one years, and after he shall have resided five years within the United States, be admitted as a citizen, without having made the usual declaration three years previous to his admission; but this declaration must be made at the time of his admission, and he must declare to the court on oath, and prove that for three years next preceding, it has been his intention to become a citizen of the United States.

When an alien, who shall have complied with the provisions of paragraph four, of this chapter, relative to declaring his intention, shall die before being naturalized, his widow and children shall be considered citizens of the United States, and entitled to all the privileges as such, upon taking the oath prescribed by law.

Aliens having borne any hereditary title, or been of any of the orders of nobility in the Kingdom or State from which they came, must renounce such title, or order of nobility, before they can be admitted as citizens of the United States.

When at war with another nation, the United States government will not admit to citizenship, the citizens, subjects, or denizens of such nation.

As to the provisions of law concerning aliens residing in the United States prior to 1812, the student is referred to the abstract of the laws of the United States, to be found at page XVI of the introduction to the Revised Statutes of Ohio, by Swan and Critchfield; also to be found at page 100 of Curwen's Revised Statutes.

The children of naturalized persons, being under the age of twenty-one years at the time of their parents being naturalized, shall, if dwelling in the United States, be considered as citizens thereof.

Children of persons who are or have been citizens of the United States, though born elsewhere, are considered as citizens of the United States.

Any alien, of the age of twenty-one years and upwards, who has enlisted or shall enlist in the armies of the United States, either the regular or the volunteer forces, and has been, or shall be hereafter, honorably discharged, may be admitted to become a citizen of the United States, upon his petition, without any previous declaration of his intention to become a citizen of the United States; and he shall not be required to prove more than one year's residence within the United States previous to his application to become such citizen; and the court admitting such alien, shall, in addition to such proof of residence and good moral character, as is now provided by law, be satisfied, by competent proof, of such person having been honorably discharged from the service of the United States as aforesaid.

Aliens may be admitted to citizenship by any court of record having common law jurisdiction, and a seal, or clerk or *prothonotary*.

Questions—What is the right to vote called? Who are called electors? Who are electors in Ohio? What is an alien? How are aliens naturalized? What is said of residents of the United States between June 18th, 1778, and April 14th, 1802? Of alien minors who arrive in this country while under the age of eighteen years? Of the widow and children of aliens who die before being fully admitted to citizenship? Of aliens having hereditary titles, or belonging to orders of nobility? When will certain aliens not be admitted? What is said of the minor children of naturalized persons? Of children of American citizens, born in other countries? What is said of the naturalization of persons who have enlisted in the military service of the United States, and been honorably discharged? In what courts may aliens be admitted to citizenship?

CHAPTER XXVII.

ELECTIONS—HOW CONDUCTED—CHALLENGE OF PERSONS OFFERING TO VOTE.

In order that the government may be administered, it is necessary that officers should be elected for that purpose.

As the duties of some of these officers pertain to the whole State, we call them State officers; those whose duties are limited to the county we call county officers; and those whose duties are limited to and pertain to the government of the townships, cities or villages, we call township, city or village officers, as the case may be.

These officers, as well as the military officers of the State, are required, before entering upon the duties of their office, to take a solemn oath to support the constitution of the State and of the United States, and to discharge the duties of their respective offices faithfully.

State and county officers are elected on the second Tuesday of October, and city, village and township officers are elected on the first Monday of April of each year.

Questions affecting the interests of the people, other than the mere election of officers, are often voted upon and determined by them at the elections.

As a matter of covenience the State is divided into election districts or precincts. Each *ward* of a city or village composes an election district; and each of the townships, exclusive of the territory embraced within the limits of any city or village divided into wards. Some of the larger townships, however, are divided into two or more election districts.

It is necessary that judges should preside at all elections, to receive the ballots offered, and to discharge such duties in relation thereto as the law prescribes.

The electors required by law to act as judges are designated in the act of the General Assembly of 1870. See Session Laws of 1870, page 47.

Ballot-boxes are provided for each election precinct, in which the ballots of the electors are deposited.

Provision has been made by law for the holding of special elections. These may be held for the of purpose filling vacancies, occurring through the removal, resignation or death of officers, where such vacancies can not be filled by appointment; or to enable the people to vote upon measures submitted to them by some provision of law.

A ballot is a paper ticket on which is written or printed the names of the persons for whom the voter intends to vote, and the offices to which the persons named on the ballot are intended to be chosen. The law provides that "all ballots voted at any election, held in pursuance of law, shall be written on plain white paper, or printed with black ink, with a space of not less than one-fifth of an inch between each name, on plain white news printing paper, without any device or mark of any description to distinguish one ticket from another, or by which one ticket may be known from another by its appearance, except the words at the head of the ticket; and whenever any ballot, with a certain designated heading, shall contain printed thereon, in place of another, any name not found on the regular ballot having such heading, such name so found shall be regarded by the judges of election as having been placed there for the purpose of fraud, and said ballot shall not count for the name so found; and it shall be unlawful for any person to print for distribution at the polls, or distribute to any elector, or knowingly to vote any ballot printed or written contrary to the provisions of this act: Provided that nothing herein contained shall be construed to prohibit the erasure, correction or insertion of any name by pencil mark or with ink upon the face of the printed ballot."

The printed or written votes of electors upon any

question or measure submitted to them at an election, is also called a ballot.

The person offering to vote delivers his ballot to one of the judges of the election, who, as he receives it, pronounces the name of the elector. The name of each voter is entered upon poll-books kept for that purpose by clerks of the election.

The judges, or any elector qualified to vote at the election, may challenge any person offering to vote; that is, may object to such person voting, on the ground that he has not the legal qualifications entitling him to vote. When such a challenge is made, one of the judges administers an oath or affirmation to the person challenged. The form of the oath, or affirmation, is as follows:

"You do swear (or affirm) that you will fully and truly answer all such questions as shall be put to you touching your place of residence and qualifications as an elector at this election."

Thereupon the person challenged is required to answer the questions put to him touching his qualifications as an elector. If the challenge is not withdrawn, the following oath or affirmation is administered.

"You do solemnly swear (or affirm) that you are a citizen of the United States, of the age of twenty-one years; that you have been an inhabitant of this State for one year next preceding this election; that you are now an actual resident of this township (or ward) and that you have not voted at this election."

If a person challenged refuses to take the oath, or to answer fully any lawful questions put to him, his vote must be rejected. If, after an examination of the challenged party, the judges are not satisfied, they may receive other evidence, and if finally satisfied that he is not a legal voter, must reject his vote.

The supreme court of this State has held that where the judges improperly reject a proffered ballot, they are liable in an action for damages.

The judges of the election are authorized to preserve order, and may cause disorderly persons to be confined until the close of the election; and constables present are required to obey their orders in preserving the peace.

Questions—For what purpose are officers elected? In treating of the officers required to carry on the government, under what general classification do we refer to them? At what time is the general election for the State and county officers held? The election for township officers? What is said of official oaths? When are State and county officers elected? City, village, and township officers? Do the people vote for any other purpose than the election of officers? What is said of election precincts? Of judges of elections? Of ballot boxes? Of special elections? What is a ballot? What does the law require in regard to ballots? In what way do electors vote? What is meant by challenging a person who offers to vote? In what way do the judges determine whether a person challenged to vote is qualified? In what cases must the vote of a person challenged be rejected? What is said of the power of judges of election to preserve order?

CHAPTER XXVIII.

OF ELECTIONS CONTINUED—CANVASS OF VOTES AND RETURN OF POLL-BOOKS.

At the close of the election, the names on the poll-books are counted and the number set down at the foot of the poll-books, and certified to in writing thereunder, by the judges, and attested by the clerks. The ballot-boxes are then opened and the ballots taken out and inspected by the judges, one of whom is required to read, distinctly, from each ballot, the name or names therein contained.

The clerks enter in seperate columns of a tally-sheet, under the names of the persons voted for, all the votes read out by the judges.

One of the poll-books and tally-sheet are sealed and directed to the clerk of the Court of Common Pleas of the county in which the election is held, and is taken to that officer by one of the judges of the election. One of the poll-boks of a presidental election is to be returned to the clerk of the court within three days after the election; of a State or county election, within two days; of a township election, the returns must be made to the township clerk within one day.

The clerk of the Court of Common Pleas, assisted by two justices of the Peace of the county, is required to make abstracts of the returns made to him.

In case of the inability of the clerk to officiate in making the canvass, his deputy may act in his stead; and in case the office of clerk is not represented by deputy, and such clerk be absent or in anywise disqualified to serve, the probate judge of the county acts with the justices in examining the returns.

The clerk and justices, or judge and justices, (as the case may be) declare who have the highest number of votes for the county offices and for senators and representatives in the General Assembly, and the clerk issues certificates of election to such persons.

Abstracts of the votes for State officers and members of Congress are sent to the seat of government at Columbus, to the officers designated by law, who open the same, and declare who are elected. When two or more counties are joined in a senatorial, representative or judicial district, the clerk of such county or counties, of any such districts, that have a smaller population, are required to make out fair abstracts of the votes given within any such county, under the seal of the court of common pleas, and attested by the clerk, and transmit the same by a special messenger to the clerk of the court of common pleas of that county, of any such district, hav- the largest population, within ten days after the day of election, who is required to receive and open the same in the same manner as returns of election districts, and incorporate the returns from such county or counties having such smaller population, with the returns of election districts of the county having the largest population, and deliver to the persons elected certificates of their election.

Questions—At the close of an election what is required of the judges and clerks? What is said of the tally-sheets? What is required to be done with the poll-books and tally-sheets? What officers examine the returns, and make abstracts thereof? What officers declare the vote for county officers and senators and representatives? What is done with the abstracts of votes for members of Congress and State officers? How are returns made when two or more counties are embraced in one district?

CHAPTER XXIX.

HOW THE PRESIDENT AND VICE-PRESIDENT OF THE UNITED STATES ARE ELECTED.

The people do not vote directly for President and Vice-President of the United States, but the voters of each State choose a number of men equal to the number of senators and representatives to which it is entitled in Congress. These are called presidental electors. The State of Ohio is entitled to two senators and twenty representatives in Congress. Hence we choose twenty-two presidential electors.

These electors convene at the State Capital, on the first Wednesday of December next after the election, and vote for President and Vice-President, and make a list of the persons voted for, and the number of votes for each, which is sent to the president of the United States senate.

On the second Wednesday of February, the president of the senate, in presence of all the senators and representatives, opens all the certificates, and the votes are counted. The persons having a majority of all the electoral votes for President and Vice-President are declared elected.

In case a person receives a plurality of the electoral vote for President, but not a majority, the house of representatives elects a President.

Suppose there are three candidates for the office, and that of the 366 electoral votes, one candidate should receive 150 votes, another 130 votes, and the other 86. Now, a majority of 366 cannot be less than 184; consequently neither would be elected. In such case the house of representatives would elect a President, the members of each State voting by themselves, and a candidate receiving a majority of the representatives of a State, has one vote for such majority; that is, there are as many presidential votes as there are States, and the person who receives the votes of a majority of the States is elected.

If the electors fail to elect a Vice-President, the senate, in a body, chooses one from the two having the highest number of electoral votes.

Questions—How do people vote for President and Vice-President of the United States? To how many presidential electors is the State of Ohio entitled? What is done with the statement of the vote of electors? When and where is the vote of the various States counted and the result declared? In case no person receives a majority of all the votes cast for President, how is the President elected? What is the difference between a plurality and a majority? In case the electors fail to elect a Vice-President, how is that officer elected?

LEGISLATIVE DEPARTMENT.

CHAPTER XXX.

THE GENERAL ASSEMBLY, HOW ORGANIZED—ITS GENERAL POWERS AND DUTIES.

Senators and representatives are elected biennially by the electors in their respective counties or districts, on the second Tuesday of October. Their term of office commences on the first day of January next thereafter, and continues two years.

The constitution of the State provides that "senators and representatives shall have resided in their respective counties or districts one year next preceding their election, unless they shall have been absent on the public business of the United States, or of this State."

"No person holding office under the authority of the United States, or any lucrative office under the authority of this State, shall be eligible to, or have a seat in the General Assembly; but this provision shall not extend to township officers, justices of the peace, notaries public, or officers of the militia.

"No person hereafter convicted of an embezzlement of the public funds, shall hold any office in this State; nor shall any person, holding public money for disbursement, or otherwise, have a seat in the General Assembly until he shall have accounted for, and paid such money into the treasury."

All regular sessions of the General Assembly convene at the Capitol, at Columbus, on the first Monday in January, biennially.

The room in which the senators meet is called the senate chamber, and the room in which the representatives meet, is called the hall of the house of representatives.

Every senator and every representative takes an oath to support the constitution of the United States, and the constitution of the State of Ohio, and that he will faithfully discharge the duties of his office, according to the best of his ability.

A majority of each house constitutes a *quorum* for the transaction of business.

Each house determines the rules of its proceedings, and judges of the qualifications, election and returns of its members. Each house keeps a journal of its proceedings, and publishes the same.

The yeas and nays, that is, the way in which members vote on any question, must be entered on the journal, at the request of any two members; and, on the passage of every bill, in either house, the vote must be taken by yeas and nays, and entered upon the journal.

The house of representatives chooses one of its members to preside over it, who is called a speaker. The lieutenant-governor is the presiding officer of the senate, and is called the president.

The presiding officer preserves order, and sees that the business of the house is properly attended to.

When a question is to be decided by the house, the presiding officer "puts it to vote"; that is, requests the members to express their judgment ~~in favor of~~ or against the measure. Those who favor the measure say, "aye"; those who oppose it say, "no".

The officers of the senate consist of a president; clerk, and first and second assistant; sergeant-at-arms, and first and second assistants.

The officers of the house of representatives consist of a speaker; a clerk and two assistants; a sergeant-at-arms, and two assistants.

After the first two weeks of the session, either house may, on the recommendation of the clerk or sergeant-at-arms, elect or provide for the appointment of an additional clerk or clerks, sergeant or sergeants-at-arms.

Questions—When and how often are members of the General Assembly elected? When does their term of office commence, and how long does it continue? What are the provisions of the constitution concerning the eligibility of persons for a seat in the General Assembly? At what time and place does the regular session of the Assembly ~~convene~~? Name the rooms in which the two houses meet. What oath do the members take? What proportion of the members constitute a *quorum?* What is meant by the word *quorum?* What body fixes the rules and determines the qualifications and election of members? What is said of the "yeas" and "nays"? What officers preside over the General Assembly? At what time may additional officers be elected?

CHAPTER XXXI.

OF THE ENACTMENT OF LAWS—ELECTION OF UNITED STATES SENATORS.

When the two houses are organized and ready for business, the governor presents to them his message. This is a written statement of the condition of the State, and calls attention to such subjects as the governor thinks need legislation.

The presiding officers of the respective houses usually appoint committees, to whom are referred the different subjects presented for the consideration of the General Assembly. Sometimes, however, committees are elected by the house or senate, instead of being appointed by the presiding officer. These committees consider and report upon the matters referred to them.

Were it not for these committees it would be almost impossible to transact all the business presented to the General Assembly. Some measures are proposed by the governor and others by the members. The people sometimes want a law passed, and procure a paper to be drawn up containing their wishes, which is called a petition, and send it to the Assembly. Suppose this petition asks the Assembly to pass a law in regard to education; the petition is referred to the committee on education. If the petition relates to insurance, it is referred to the committee on insurance, and so on. Sometimes members or others, draw up bills which they desire to have passed.

A bill is a draft of a proposed law; or it may be defined as "an instrument presented to a legislative body for its approbation and enactment." These bills are referred to the appropriate committees. If the bills so referred are considered proper and necessary, the committee reports in favor of them and recommends that they be passed—that is, enacted into a law.

These committees frequently draft bills and report them to the house. If a committee reports against a measure referred to it, the house generally concurs with its recommendation and dismisses the subject.

It is not deemed necessary to state here all the particular forms through which a bill must pass before it can become a law. It is perhaps sufficient to say that, after it has been discussed and amended, a final vote is taken on the question: "Shall the bill pass?" If a majority of all the members vote "aye," it is passed; if not it is lost.

When a bill is passed by one house, it is sent to the other, where it is duly considered and voted upon, If it passes that house without amendment it becomes a law.

If a bill is amended in the second house, it is sent back to the house where it originated; and when both houses finally agree, the bill becomes a law.

The General Assembly elects United States senators.

Each State is entitled to two senators, who are elected for the term of six years.

Questions—When the two houses of the Assembly are organized, what duty does the governor perform? What is said of the appointment of committees? What are the duties of these committees? What is a bill? When a bill is introduced, what course is usually pursued with reference to it? In case a member wishes to introduce a bill, what does he do? When a bill is passed in one house, what is done with it? What members of Congress are elected by the General Assembly?

EXECUTIVE DEPARTMENT.

CHAPTER XXXII.

EXECUTIVE POWER, WHERE VESTED—DUTIES OF THE GOVERNOR, LIEUTENANT-GOVERNOR, AND SECRETARY OF STATE.

While by the constitution, the executive department of the State consists of a governor, lieutenant-governor, secretary of state, auditor, treasurer, and attorney-general, the supreme executive power is vested in the governor. Each of these officers, except the auditor, holds his office for two years. The auditor holds his office for four years.

The governor is commander-in chief of the military and naval forces of the State, and may call out such forces to execute the laws, to suppress insurrections, and to repel invasions. He transacts all necessary business for the State with the officers of the government. He may convene the General Assembly on extraordinary occasions. He informs the General Assembly of such measures as he deems expedient.

He may grant reprieves, commutations, and pardons

for all offenses except treason and cases of impeachment. If a person has been found guilty of an offense and is sentenced to be punished, the governor has power to postpone or put off the time when the punishment shall commence. This is called a *reprieve*. If he should set the person free and discharge him from punishment, this would be called a *pardon*.

By *commutation* is meant the change of a punishment to which a person has been condemned, into a less severe one.

When a person is convicted of treason, the governor may suspend the execution of the sentence, and report the case to the General Assembly, at its next meeting, when the General Assembly shall either pardon, commute the sentence, direct its execution, or grant a further reprieve.

The lieutenant-governor is, by virtue of his office, president of the senate, and in case of the impeachment of the governor, his removal from office, death, inability, resignation, or absence from the State, the duties of the office devolve upon the lieutenant-governor.

The secretary of state is required, among other things, to take charge of the laws and resolutions passed by the General Assembly; to provide copies, and to attend to the printing of the laws; to countersign and register commissions; to procure and transmit seals for courts; to procure fuel and stationery for the use of the State; to take charge of the field-notes, maps, records, documents, papers and implements relating to the surveys of the public lands within the State of Ohio, which have been delivered to the executive of the State by the surveyor of the United States, at Detroit, by order of the General Government of the United States.

Questions—In whom is the executive department vested? State their terms of office. In what officer is the supreme executive power of the State vested? What relation does the governor sustain to the military and naval forces of the State? Enumerate other duties and powers of the governor. What is a reprieve? Pardon? Commutation? What may the governor do in relation to a conviction for treason? What is said of the lieutenant-governor? Enumerate some of the duties of the secretary of state.

CHAPTER XXXIII.

OF STATE OFFICERS AND THEIR DUTIES CONTINUED—AUDITOR—TREASURER—ATTORNEY-GENERAL—COMPTROLLER OF THE TREASURY—CLERK OF THE SUPREME COURT.

Among the many duties the auditor is required to perform, the following may be mentioned: He is to examine and adjust accounts and claims against the State; to keep accounts between the treasurer and the State; to report to the General Assembly a statement of the receipts, disbursements and condition of the treasury; to transmit to the county auditors a list of the lands within their counties subject to taxation; to furnish forms and instructions to county auditors concerning the assessing, charging, collecting and accounting for the public revenue.

The State treasurer has charge of the public moneys

that are paid into the State treasury. He is required to pay warrants drawn on the treasury by the auditor of the State, duly certified and countersigned by the comptroller; and to keep accurate records of the number, amount, and date of every draft of the comptroller, in favor of the treasurer of state, and to whom payable, as well as of every warrant of the auditor of state on the treasurer, presented and paid.

The attorney-general is the law officer of the State. The following are some of his duties: He is to prosecute and defend for the State, in actions in the supreme court; and in other courts when required by the governor or General Assembly; to prosecute the official bonds of all delinquent officers in which the State may be interested; to conduct prosecutions against persons for exercising an office or franchise unlawfully; to give his opinion and legal advice to State officers, the General Assembly, and to prosecuting attorneys, when requested.

The comptroller of the treasury holds his office for three years. He is required to collect from contractors the amount due the State for convict labor; to draw, in favor of the treasurer, upon delinquent banks, for taxes assessed. The comptroller and auditor are required to examine all claims presented for payment out of the State treasury, and must be satisfied that the claim is just and legal, and ought to be paid, before they allow and audit, or certify, countersign, or register the same. When moneys are to be paid into the treasury, the comptroller certifies to the treasurer the amount to be paid, and the fund to which the same shall belong. It is his duty to make dilligent inquiry after all claims and accounts in favor of the State, and require prompt payment of the same; to make (assisted by the auditor) quarterly settlements with the State treasurer, and to report the result to the governor.

The duties of the State commissioner of common schools will be considered in the chapters on education.

The clerk of the supreme court holds his term of office for three years. It is his duty to enter and record the orders, decrees and judgments of the court, and to perform such other duties as by law and the rules of the court may be required of him.

Questions—What is said of the duties of State auditor? Of the State treasurer? Of the attorney-general? Of the comptroller of the treasury? Of the clerk of the supreme court?

CHAPTER XXXIV.

OF CERTAIN BOARDS AND COMMISSIONERS—BOARD OF PUBLIC WORKS—OF STATE CHARITIES—COMMISSIONERS OF THE SINKING FUND—BOARD OF AGRICULTURE—COMMISSIONERS OF RAILROADS AND TELEGRAPHS—SUPERINTENDENT OF INSURANCE—STATE LIBRARY COMMISSIONERS—COMMISSIONERS AND AGENTS OF EMMIGRATION—COMMISSIONERS OF FISHERIES—NOTARIES PUBLIC.

The word *board* is used to designate a body of persons whose duty it is to manage or control some institution, or to discharge certain specific duties.

Provision has been made by law for the establishment of various boards, to discharge duties in which the people of the whole State are more or less interested.

It is frequently the case that for the discharge of particular duties, a single person is employed, called a commissioner. If two or more are employed, we refer to them as a board, or board of commissioners. Some of these commissioners or boards are appointed by the governor; others are elected by the people, while some of them are designated by name in the law creating the office and prescribing the duties thereof.

Some of the State boards are composed of State officers, who, in addition to their other duties, are required by law to act together in managing and controlling certain public interests. Trustees and directors of the various charitable, benevolent, penal and reformatory institutions of the State, may, with propriety, be called boards.

The following will indicate briefly the duties of some of these boards and commissioners:

The board of public works consists of three members, elected by the people. Their term of office is three years, the expiration of which is so arranged that one member is elected each year at the October election.

This board has the control and management of the public works of the State. These works are divided into divisions, and each member of the board takes charge of a separate division.

The following are the principal public works of the State: the Ohio canal, Walhonding canal, Hocking canal,

Miami and Erie canal, Western Reserve and Maumee road, National road and the Muskingum improvement.

The board of State charities consists of five persons appointed by the governor. This board is required to investigate the whole system of the public charitable and correctional institutions of the State, and to recommend such changes and additional provisions as they may deem necessary for their economical and efficient administration. They receive no compensation for their services, except their actual traveling expenses.

The auditor of state, the secretary of state and attorney-general constitute a board of commissioners styled "the commissioners of the sinking fund." This board attends to the payment of the public debt and interest, according to the provisions of law for that purpose.

The State board of agriculture consists of ten members, who are elected for the term of two years. This board, together with the president of each county agricultural society, or other delegate therefrom, duly authorized, is required to hold an annual meeting at the city of Columbus, for the purpose of deliberation and consultation, as to the wants, prospects, and condition of the agricultural interests throughout the State. At such meeting the reports from the county society are delivered to the president of the State board. The president and delegates elect the members of the State board.

The governor, by and with the consent of the senate, appoints a commissioner of railroads and telegraphs. It is the duty of this officer to report violations of the railroad laws; to inspect and examine any and all tracks and bridges which he may have reason to believe are defective, and to notify the superintendent or other proper officer, of the condition thereof, and of the repairs required; and he may prescribe the rate of speed of passing trains over any dangerous or defective track, bridge, or other structure, until the repairs are made; or he may wholly stop the running of passenger trains over such defective track, bridge or other structure. It is also his duty to ascertain and report to the governor on or before the first of January of each year, the condition of all the railroad and telegraph companies having lines in this State, and also the particulars of all the accidents resulting in injuries to persons upon railroads.

The law provides for the appointment of a State board of school examiners. Their duties will be considered in the chapters on education.

An insurance department has been established, charged with the execution of the laws in relation to insurance and insurance companies.

The chief officer of this department is a superintendent, appointed by the governor, who holds his office for three years.

The governor, secretary of state and state librarian constitute a board of commissioners for the management of the State library.

The librarian is appointed by the governor and holds his office for two years.

Provision is made by law authorizing the governor to appoint a commissioner and two agents to encourage immigration to this State.

By the statute of 1873 the governor is required to appoint three commissioners of fisheries, whose duties are prescribed in section two of the act, as follows:

"It shall be the duty of the commissioners to examine the various rivers, lakes, ponds, and streams of the State of Ohio, and the waters adjoining the same, with a view of ascertaining whether they can be rendered more productive of fish, and what measures are desirable to effect this object, either in restoring the production of fish in them, or in protecting, or propagating the fish that at present frequent them, or otherwise. Said commissioners shall inquire into the matter of the artificial propagation of fish in the various waters throughout the State; and such commissioners shall report the result of their labors, and any recommendations they may have to offer, at the next meeting of the General Assembly of this State."

Notaries public are appointed by the governor. They are authorized to take the proof and acknowledgement of deeds and other instruments; to administer oaths; to take affidavits and depositions; to demand acceptance of bills of exchange and of promissory notes, and to protest the same for non-acceptance or non-payment.

Questions—What is the word *board* used to designate? For what purposes are boards established? What is said of boards and commissioners? Of the board of public works? Name the principal public works of the State. What is said of the board of state charities? Of commissioners of the sinking fund? Of the State board of agriculture? Of the commissioner of railroads and telegraphs? Of the insurance department? Of State library commissioners? Of commissioners of immigration? Of commissioners of fisheries? Of notories public?

CHAPTER XXXV.

OF COUNTIES AND COUNTY OFFICERS.

As it would be impossible for the State officers whose duties we have considered, to transact all the public business necessary for the people, the State has been subdivided into smaller portions of territory, each of which has a government, not inconsistent with that of the State. Of these subdivisions, the largest, for the purposes of government, are counties.

Most of the county officers are elected by the people.

The probate judge holds his office for five years; county commissioners, recorder, clerk of the court of common pleas and the surveyor for three years; the sheriff, auditor, coronor, treasurer and prosecuting attorney for two years.

By the law of 1873 the probate judge of each county is required to appoint a county board of school examiners to consist of three persons—one for the term of one year, one for two years, and one for three years and annually thereafter, one for three years, so that their term of office shall be for three years.

Provision is made by law for the establishment of county courts and the election of county judges in some of the counties.

Each county has a county seat or seat of justice; that is, a place where the public business is transacted. A court-house, jail, and offices for the county officers, is necessary at the seat of justice.

Questions—What are the largest subdivisions of the State for the purposes of government? Name the county officers? For what length of time are county officers elected or appointed? What is said of the appointment of examiners? Of seats of justice?

CHAPTER XXXVI.

COUNTY COMMISSIONERS — CLERK OF THE COURT OF COMMON PLEAS — SHERIFF — CORONER — COUNTY AUDITOR—TREASURER—RECORDER OF DEEDS—SURVEYOR—PROSECUTING ATTORNEY—GAUGERS AND INSPECTORS.

The county commissioners are required under certain limitations, to look after and have a general superintendence over the interests and property of the county. Among other things they have authority to sell or dispose of any real estate, under certain restrictions, belonging to the county, when, in their judgment, the public interests would be promoted thereby. They may also purchase property for the use of the county; appropriate lands for a court-house site or a site for a jail; provide for the reconstruction of bridges that may have been burned by proximity to railroad tracks, and may aid in rebuilding, at the expense of the county, bridges owned by plank road companies; may offer and pay rewards out of the county treasury for the detection and apprehension of persons charged with or convicted of crimes or offenses made punishable by death or imprisonment in the penitentiary by the laws of the State.

The duties of probate judge will be noticed in a subsequent chapter, when treating of the judicial department.

The clerk of the court of common pleas keeps the records and papers pertaining to the common pleas court. He has power to administer oaths or affirmations, to take and certify to acknowledgments of deeds, mortgages, liens, powers of attorney and other instruments of writing. He also acts in conjunction with certain other officers, in canvassing and making abstracts of election returns.

The sheriff has the charge and custody of the jails in his county, and of the prisoners of the same. He is to preserve the public peace and to apprehend offenders. He is required to execute all warrants, writs and other process to him directed by proper and lawful authority; to attend upon all courts of common pleas, and district courts of his county, during their session. In the execution of his duties he is authorized and required to call to his aid such person or persons, or power of the county as may be necessary.

It is the duty of a coroner, when informed that a person has died suddenly, or from violence, to procure six men to act as jurors, and with them he is to investigate and inquire into the cause and circumstances of the death. This investigation is called a coroner's inquest.

Coroners are required by law to discharge the duties of sheriff, when the sheriff is a party interested.

The county auditor is by law clerk to the board of county commissioners, and keeps a record of their proceedings. He is required to keep an account current with the treasurer. Certain claims against the county, after having been allowed by the commissioners are paid upon the auditor's warrant. It is his duty to furnish assessors with the list of lands within his county subject to taxation, and when an alteration of the lists of lands becomes necessary, in order to indicate to whom the tax thereon shall be charged, it is his duty to make the proper transfer. The duties of the auditor will be further considered when treating of the levy and collection of taxes.

It is the duty of the county treasurer to collect and receive the moneys required to be raised in his county to defray the expenses of the State, county and township governments, and to pay the same out in the manner prescribed by law.

The county recorder provides, at the expense of the county, suitable blank books, which he keeps in his office at the county-seat, and in which he copies or records all the deeds mortgages, and other papers which by law it is proper to record in his office, that may be presented to him.

The object of recording these documents is that they may be preserved, and to give notice to all persons interested, of their existence.

In order to determine the location and boundary lines of lands, provision has been made by law for the election of a county surveyor, who, when applied to by any party in interest, or when ordered by the court, is required to make and execute surveys within his county. He is required to keep a record of all official surveys.

It is the duty of the prosecuting attorney to prosecute for and in behalf of the State all complaints, suits and controversies in which the State is a party, within his county, in the district court, in the court of common pleas, and in the probate court.

For the purpose of preventing the adulteration of certain articles of commerce, and to secure honesty and fair dealing in relation to the quality and quantity thereof, the court of common pleas is authorized to appoint in each county one gauger and inspector of domestic and foreign spirits, linseed oil, lard oil and coal oil; one inspector of flour, meal and buckwheat; one inspector of beef, pork, lard and butter; one inspector of pot and pearl ashes. Inspectors of provisions and other merchandise are required to examine and inspect the provisions and merchandise of those who keep and offer them for sale, and to affix a brand or mark to such articles, so that purchasers may be advised as to what they purchase.

The law provides for the appointment of fish inspectors in the counties bordering on Lake Erie. In 1834 an act was passed by the General Assembly providing for the election of inspectors of merchandise in the county of Montgomery, by the people. In 1867 an act was passed providing that on the application of five or more citizens of any county in this State where mineral oils are refined, produced or sold for illuminating purposes, the court of common pleas shall appoint inspectors thereof.

Appropriate penalties are provided for the punishment of those who violate inspection laws.

The duties of school examiners will be considered in another chapter.

Questions—What is said of the general powers and duties of county commissioners? Specify some of them. What is said of the duties and powers of the clerk of the court of common pleas? Of the sheriff? Coroner? County auditor? County treasurer? County recorder? County surveyor? Prosecuting attorney? Of the appointment and duties of inspectors and gaugers?

CHAPTER XXXVII.

OF TOWNSHIPS AND TOWNSHIP OFFICERS—TRUSTEES—CLERK—TREASURER—ASSESSORS—CONSTABLES—SUPERVISORS OF ROADS.

Each organized township has a government of its own, and its people elect officers to administer such government, to discharge certain duties for the good of the people.

No new township can be organized with less than twenty-two square miles of territory, unless it includes a city or an incorporated village.

All townships are capable of suing or being sued in any court of this State, and may acquire by devise, bequest or deed of gift, and hold property for the benefit of the township.

The law provides for the holding of annual meetings in each township, on the first Monday of April in each year, at which time the following officers are elected: Three trustees, a justice or justices of the peace, a township clerk, a treasurer, an assessor, as many constables as have been determined upon by the trustees, a supervisor of roads for each road district, and a supervisor of ditches.

Their term of office continues for one year, except justices of the peace, who hold their offices for three years.

Among the duties required of trustees may be mentioned the following: To act as election boards; to bind out and protect apprentices; to levy taxes for township purposes in certain cases; to establish and protect cemeteries; to locate and establish ditches; to settle disputes in relation to division fences; to select jurors and return a list of the same to the clerk of the court of common pleas; to furnish relief to poor persons and paupers; to open, vacate, establish and alter roads.

The number of justices of the peace for each township is determined by the court of common pleas. This number, however, may be increased or diminished by an order of the probate court, when circumstances seem to require it. The duties of justices will be considered when treating of the judiciary.

The township clerk keeps a record of the proceedings of the trustees of the accounts allowed and adjusted by them; furnishes certificates of the election of township officers, and keeps an account of the receipts and expenditures of the township, and of the board of education.

It is the duty of the township treasurer to receive and take charge of all moneys which by law are to be paid into the township treasury.

The assessors are required to make and return to the county auditors, lists and valuations of all the taxable property in their respective townships, wards and assessment districts; also statements of the number of sheep killed and injured by dogs. They are required to take and return to the county auditors an enumeration of all deaf and dumb, blind, insane and idiotic persons in their township, ward or district, every four years. They are also required, every fourth year, to take an enumeration of all the male inhabitants above the age of twenty-one years, residing within their jurisdiction, and return the same to the clerk of the court of common pleas.

The number of constables to be elected in each township is determined by the trustees.

Constables are ministerial officers of justices of the peace. A ministerial officer is one who acts under the authority of a superior, and does what his superior orders him to do. They are required to post up warrants for elections, serve copies of election lists, to make complaint against persons violating the gambling act, to arrest, on view or warrant, and bring to justice all felons and disturbers and violaters of the criminal laws of this State, and to suppress all riots, affrays and unlawful assemblies. In discharging their duties constables may call to their aid the power of the county, or such assistance as may be necessary.

It is the duty of supervisors of roads to open, or cause to be opened, the public roads in their respective districts, (except such as are by law exempt from their care), and to superintend the work thereon as required by law, to keep the same in repair.

The supervisors have no jurisdiction, for the purposes of opening or repair, over roads in cities and villages, nor over township roads, except such as are thirty feet wide and commence in a State, turnpike, county, or township road, and pass on and intersect another State, turnpike, county, or township road; nor over turnpike and plank roads, except free turnpikes.

In each township through which any ditch, drain, or water-course shall have been constructed, it is the duty of the electors at the spring election, each year, to elect a supervisor of ditches, who is required to see that such ditches, drains, or water-courses are kept open and in good repair.

Questions—What is said in the lesson in relation to the organization of new townships? Of their corporate powers? Of the election of township officers? Of their term of office? What is said of the duties of trustees? Of the number of justices of the peace in each township? Mention some of the duties of the township clerk. Of treasurer. Of assessors. What is said as to the number of constables? Of their relations to justices of the peace? Mention their duties. What is required of supervisors of roads? What is said of their jurisdiction? Of the election and duties of supervisors of ditches?

CHAPTER XXXVIII.

CITIES AND VILLAGES.

Where a large number of houses and inhabitants are established in one place, it is found necessary for the preservation of good order, and for the purpose of making those public improvements essential for the convenience and comfort of the people, to exercise powers of government not conferred upon townships; and therefore the people of such places are authorized by law to unite in a body politic, and when so united their corporations are known as cities or villages.

In respect to the exercise of certain corporate powers and to the number, character, power and duties of certain officers, these corporations are divided into cities of the first, and cities of the second class; incorporated villages, and incorporated villages for special purposes.

Cities having a population of over twenty thousand are deemed cities of the first class; those with less than that number, cities of the second class.

The law provides that no city of the second class shall be advanced to the grade of a city of the first class, until it shall have attained a population of twenty thousand.

No incorporated village shall be advanced to the grade of a city of the second class until it shall have attained a population of five thousand.

No incorporated village for special purposes shall be advanced to the grade of an incorporated village until it shall have obtained a population of five hundred.

No village shall be incorporated with a less number of inhabitants than five hundred.

All municipal corporations are vested with certain general powers; may sue and be sued, contract and be contracted with, and may hold and possess property, real and personal.

The powers conferred upon these corporations differ according to their grade; greater powers and privileges being conferred upon municipalities of the higher class or grade.

When a large number of persons are assembled together, as in our large cities, their wants and necessities are more diversified, and their relative rights and duties more difficult to adjust, and hence the necessity for conferring greater powers upon the government of such localities.

As certain rules and regulations which could not be anticipated by the General Assembly, are found necessary in cities and villages, limited legislative powers are conferred upon them, which is exercised by a body elected by the people, known as trustees, councilmen, or aldermen.

The cities are divided into wards or districts for the sake of convenience, each ward being entitled to be represented in the government of the city.

Each municipality has a chief executive officer, called a mayor, and such other subordinate officers as are authorized by law, to superintend the interests of the municipality, and to preserve good order therein.

Questions—What is said as to the organization of cities and villages, and the necessity therefor? Their classification? Of their general powers? Are their powers equal? Why not? What is said of their legislative powers? Of wards? Of officers?

JUDICIAL DEPARTMENT.

CHAPTER XXXIX.

ESTABLISHMENT OF COURTS—THE SUPREME COURT AND ITS JURISDICTION.

As people often fail to agree with regard to their relative rights and duties, and as they sometimes violate their agreements with each other, and even violate and disobey those rules and regulations prescribed for their conduct, it is necessary that tribunals should be provided to administer justice, to determine and declare the rights of parties, to investigate and decide whether the laws are observed or violated, and to declare and pronounce judgment according to law and the just deserts of the citizen. These determinations are called judicial.

By the constitution of the State, the judicial power is vested in a supreme court, in district courts, courts of common pleas, courts of probate, justices of the peace, and in such other courts, inferior to the supreme court, as the General Assembly may establish.

The supreme court consists of five judges, who hold their office for the term of five years.

The original jurisdiction of this court is limited to cases in *quo warranto*, *mandamus*, *habeas corpus*, and *procedendo*.

Quo warranto means, "by what authority."

It is the name of a writ against a person who has taken possession of an office or franchise and continues to hold possession thereof wrongfully. When the right of a person to act in an official capacity is questioned, proceedings are had in the supreme court to determine his right to the office; and this is called a proceeding in *quo warranto*.

The General Assembly sometimes confers upon associations or individuals, authority to do certain acts, which without such authority they could not do. And where parties assume to do these acts without such authority, they may be proceeded against in *quo warranto*.

Mandamus means to order or command. It is the name of a writ issued to any inferior tribunal, corporation, board, or person to compel the performance of an act which the law enjoins as a duty resulting from an office, trust or station.

Habeas corpus is from the Latin, and means, "you may have the body," or, "that you have the body." In law it is a writ designed to bring a party before a court or judge; especially one to enquire into the cause of a person's imprisonment, or detention by another, with the view to protect the rights of personal liberty.

Procedendo is the name of a writ by which a cause which has been removed from an inferior to a superior court, is sent down again to the same court to be proceeded in there, where it appears to the superior court that it was removed on insufficient grounds.

The constitution limits the original jurisdiction of the supreme court to the four great writs we have just been considering. The General Assembly, however, has authority to confer appellate jurisdiction upon it.

The statute provides that the supreme court when in session shall have power to issue writs of error and *certiorari* in criminal cases, and *supersedeas* in any case, and all other writs which may be necessary to enforce the due administration of justice throughout the State.

Certiorari is the name of a writ commanding an inferior court to certify and return the record of its proceedings to a higher court.

Supersedeas means to suspend, set aside, or stay. In law it is a writ or command to suspend the powers of an officer in certain cases, or stay proceedings under another writ.

When the supreme court is not in session, either of its judges have power to grant writs of *certiorari*, *habeas corpus*, and *supersedeas*.

The appellate jurisdiction of the supreme court, that is, the jurisdiction by virtue of which that court takes cognizance of appeals from inferior tribunals, extends only to the judgments and decrees of courts created and organized in pursuance of the provisions of the constitution.

The judge whose term of office first expires, who was not elected to fill a vacancy, is the chief justice of the court.

The supreme court is required by the constitution to hold at least one term each year. Its sessions are held at Columbus.

Questions—For what purposes are judicial tribunals provided? In what courts is the judicial power of the State vested? Of how many judges is the supreme court composed? What is their term of office? What original jurisdiction has the court? What is meant by *quo warranto*? In what cases is the writ employed? Mention some of the cases wherein *quo warranto* proceedings are had? What is meant by *mandamus*? For what purpose is the writ used? What is the meaning of *habeas corpus*? What is the office of the writ? What is *procedendo*? Has the supreme court any other than original jurisdiction? What writs may be issued by the supreme court? What is meant by *certiorari*? By *supersedeas*? For what purpose is the writ used? What writs may the judges grant, during vacation? What is meant by appellate jurisdiction? To what does the appellate jurisdiction of the supreme court extend? What judge is chief justice? How often, and at what place, are the terms of the supreme court held?

CHAPTER XL.

OF DISTRICT, COMMON PLEAS, PROBATE, SUPERIOR, AND MUNICIPAL COURTS.

The State is divided into nine common pleas districts. Each of these districts has from one to five judges, whose term of office continues for five years.

The district court consists of the judges of the common pleas of their respective districts, and one of the judges of the supreme court.

For the purposes of the district courts the nine common pleas districts are divided into five judicial circuits.

The district court is held annually once in each county. This court has the same original jurisdiction as the supreme court.

Appeals may be taken from the common pleas to the district court from all final judgments, orders or decrees in civil actions, in which the parties have not the right to demand a trial by jury; and orders dissolving injunctions in certain cases.

The district courts have power in certain cases to allow injunctions and to appoint receivers.

The courts of common pleas have original jurisdiction in all civil cases, both at law and in equity, where the sum or matter in dispute exceeds the jurisdiction of justices of the peace and appellate jurisdiction from the decision of county commissioners, justices of the peace, and other inferior courts in the proper county, in all civil cases; also of all crimes and offences except in cases of minor offences, the exclusive jurisdiction of which is invested in justices of the peace, or that may be invested in courts inferior to the common pleas. It also has jurisdiction in cases of divorce and alimony.

Three terms of the court of common pleas are usually held in each county each year.

Probate courts are established in each county. Their duties pertain chiefly to the settlement of the estates of deceased persons, though some other powers are conferred on this court by law.

Persons often have reduced to writing what disposition they wish made of their property, and what they desire to be done after their death. This writing the person signs his name to, or authorizes some one else to sign it for him in his presence; and at his request, two other persons sign their names to the instrument as witnesses. This instrument is called a will. A will, therefore, is "the legal declaration of a man's intentions of what he wills to be performed after his death." A will is sometimes called a testament.

These wills are proved before and recorded in the probate court.

Probate courts have jurisdiction in the appointment of guardians, and are required to direct and control their conduct, and to settle their accounts; to grant marriage licenses, and licenses to ministers of the gospel to solemnize marriages; to make inquests respecting lunatics, insane persons, idiots, and deaf and dumb persons, subject by law to guardianship; to make inquests of the amount of compensation to be made to the owners of real estate, when appropriated, by any corporation legally authorized to make such appropriation; and to try contests of election of justices of the peace.

Probate courts have power to administer oaths; to take acknowledgments of instruments required by law to be acknowledged; and to take depositions.

They may exercise jurisdiction in the sale of lands on petition by executors, administrators and guardians, and the assignment of dower in cases of sale; in the completion of real contracts on petition of executors and administrators; and may issue writs of *habeas corpus*, and inquire into and determine the validity of the caption and detention of persons brought before them on such writs.

Jurisdiction is conferred upon probate courts in some of the counties in this State, of certain crimes and misdemeanors, and provision is made by law regulating the practice before the court in such cases.

In some of the larger cities of the State, "superior courts" have been established, whose jurisdiction within their respective cities is nearly the same as that of the common pleas.

Other courts of limited jurisdiction are also established in cities and villages, whose duties are chiefly confined to causes growing out of alleged violations of the laws or ordinances of their respective municipalities.

Some of these municipal courts have jurisdiction similar to that of justices of the peace.

Questions—Into how many common pleas districts is the State divided? How many judges are there for each common pleas district? What is their term of office? Of what judges is the district court composed? How many circuits are there in the State for the district courts? How often is the district court held? What is said of the jurisdiction of the district courts? Of common pleas courts? How often are the terms of the common pleas court held? What court is established in each county? To what do the duties of the probate court chiefly pertain? What is a will, and what is said of it? What is said of the jurisdiction of probate courts? Of the establishment and jurisdiction of other courts?

CHAPTER XLI.

JUSTICES OF THE PEACE AND THEIR JURISDICTION — POLICE JUDGES AND MAYORS.

The jurisdiction of justices of the peace ~~in civil cases~~ is, with a few exceptions, limited to the townships in which they reside. They, ~~however~~, have authority co-extensive with their respective counties, among other things, to administer oaths; to take acknowledgments of instruments of writing; to solemnize marriages; to issue subpœnas for witnesses in matters pending before them; to try actions for forcible entry and detention of real property; to issue attachments and proceed against the effects and goods of debtors in certain cases; and to act in the absence of the probate judge in the trial of contested elections of justices of the peace.

Under certain restrictions, "justices of the peace shall have exclusive original jurisdiction of any sum not exceeding one hundred dollars and concurrent jurisdiction with the court of common pleas in any sum over one hundred dollars and not exceeding three hundred dollars."

In the following cases justices have no jurisdiction:

1. To recover damages for an assault, or assault and battery; or

2. In any action for malicious prosecution; or

3. In actions against justices of the peace or other officers for misconduct in office, except in certain cases provided for by law; or

4. In actions for slander, verbal or written; or

5. In actions on contracts for real estate; or

6. In actions in which the title to real estate is sought to be recovered or may be drawn in question, except actions of trespass on real estate, which are provided for by law.

Justices of the peace, mayors and police judges, are conservators of the peace and may issue warrants for the apprehension of any person accused of crime, and require the accused to enter into a recognizance with security, or in default of bail commit him to jail to answer before the proper court for the offense. Persons accused of offenses punishable by fine or imprisonment in the jail, brought before a magistrate on complaint of the injured party and who plead guilty, may be sentenced by the magistrate or be required to appear before the proper court for trial.

Questions.—Within what territory is the jurisdiction of a justice of the peace limited? In what matters is their jurisdiction co-extensive with the county? What is said of their original and their concurrent jurisdiction? In what cases have justices no jurisdiction? What is said of the jurdisdiction of justices, police judges and mayors, in criminal cases? When may a magistrate render final judgment in criminal cases?

CHAPTER XLII.

OF PROCEEDINGS IN JUSTICES' COURTS—TRIALS, JUDGMENTS AND EXECUTIONS.

A civil action is "a legal demand of one's right, or it is the form given by law for the recovery of that which is due."

Civil actions before justices of the peace are commenced by summons, or by the appearance and agreement of the parties without summons.

Where it appears by affidavit that the defendant is guilty of certain frauds, the justice may issue an order of arrest to bring the defendant into court.

At the time of issuing a summons, or afterward, an attachment may be issued against the goods and chattels of the defendant, when the circumstances are such as the law deems justifiable in order to secure the plaintiff's claim. These facts and circumstances must be made to appear by affidavit.

The student is referred to the statutes, Swan and Critchfield, 773, for particulars as to commencement of suits, service and return of process, and proceedings in arrest and attachment.

In case a person has in his possession property which he has no right to keep, the person who has a right to it, if the property does not exceed in value three hundred dollars, may apply to a justice for a writ to authorize the constable to take and deliver such property to the plaintiff. If the value of the property is less than one hundred dollars, justices have exclusive jurisdiction; from one hundred to three hundred, concurrent jurisdiction with the court of common pleas. The writ is called a writ of replevin, and after it is executed the parties have a trial before the justice, to determine who has the right to the possession of the property. If the plaintiff fails, he must return the property to the defendant, or pay him the value of it.

In whatever way a suit is commenced, a trial must be had, to determine the rights of the parties.

Either party may manage his own case before the justice, or may have an attorney for that purpose. Before proceeding to the trial, the parties put in their pleadings; that is, make a statement of their claims. These statements should be in writing. Making these statements ~~we call~~, "joining issue." When this is accomplished, the justice proceeds to try the issue. Those persons who know about the matters in difference between the parties are called as witnesses. Before they are permitted to testify, they are required to take a solemn oath or affirmation to testify truthfully. The oath is administered substantially as follows:

The witnesses are required to raise their right hands, and the justice then says "you [and each of you] do solemnly swear in the presence of Almighty God, the searcher of all hearts, that the testimony you shall give to the court [and jury] in the cause now in hearing, wherein John Doe is plaintiff, and Richard Roe is defendant, shall be the truth, the whole truth, and nothing but the truth, as you will answer to God."

Some people think it wrong to take an oath. In such case, when they are required to give testimony, they *affirm*.

The affirmation is administered by the justice, as follows: "You [and each of you] do solemnly declare and affirm that the testimony you shall give to the court [and jury] in the cause now in hearing, wherein A. B. is plaintiff, and C. D. is defendant, shall be the truth, the whole truth, and nothing but the truth; and this you do under the pains and penalties of perjury."

After the witnesses have made their statements, and answered all proper questions put to them, and the parties or their attorneys have argued the case to the justice, he decides it, if there is no jury, and records his judgment in a book kept for that purpose, called his docket.

Whenever a suit is commenced before a justice of the peace, either party desiring it may have it tried by a jury.

A jury in a justice court consists of six men, who are required to sit together before the justice and hear the proofs and allegations of the parties. They take an oath to discharge their duties faithfully. The justice decides what testimony is proper to be submitted to the jury. After the parties have introduced all their evidence, and have said, either in person or by attorney, what they desire to say to the jury, by way of argument, the jury, under charge of a constable, retire to another room, and there talk the matter over and agree upon a decision; and when they have thus agreed, they return into court and inform the justice what conclusion they have arrived at. This decision is called a verdict, and means a true saying. If the jury fail to agree, the justice calls another jury, if required by either party, who proceed to try the case, unless the parties consent that the justice may render judgment on the evidence already given.

When the jurors have agreed upon their verdict, the justice makes a record of their decision in his journal, and renders his judgment thereon.

In procuring a jury, the justice writes down the names of eighteen good men of the township, and each party strikes off or rejects six of the persons named on the list, and those whose names remain, constitute the jury, who are summoned to appear before the justice.

After judgment has been rendered in any case, it is necessary that it should be enforced. This is done by the constable, who acts by authority of a written order issued by the justice, called an execution. Suppose a judgment is rendered in favor of a party for a sum of money: the justice issues his execution, in which he commands the constable to levy upon the property of the party against whom the judgment was rendered, and to sell enough to pay the debt and costs, and to bring the money to the justice to be paid to the party entitled thereto.

To enable persons against whom judgments are rendered in justices' courts, to pay the same without sacrificing their property, provision is made for the stay of execution; so that, with the exception of a few cases, (see statutes, Swan and Critchfield, 797) by giving security for the payment of the judgment, the issuing of the execution may be postponed, as follows: On judgments for five dollars and under, for 60 days; over five and under twenty dollars, 90 days; for twenty dollars and under fifty dollars, 150 days; for fifty dollars or upwards, 240 days. When judgment is obtained against a surety who takes a stay and obtains a judgment against a principal, stay of execction can be allowed on the judgment against the principal only so long that the stay will expire one month before that allowed to the surety, on the judgment against him.

A removal of the cause to the court of common pleas is provided for by law, when it is conceived justice has not been done. In some instances the case is thus removed when a party thinks the proceedings, or some of them, before the justice, were not according to law. In all cases not otherwise specially provided for, appeals may be taken from justices' courts to the court of common pleas.

The law, in its humanity, exempts from execution or sale for any debt, damage, fine, or amercement, such property of every person who has a family as is necessary for the comfort of the family. [See statutes, Swan and Critchfield, 1043, for property exempt.]

Questions—What is a civil action? How are actions commenced before a justice of the peace? When may an order of arrest be issued? An attachment? What is said of actions in replevin? How are the rights of the parties determined? What is meant by joining issue? What do we call the persons who are called to testify in a case? What is said of the oath? Of the affirmation? Of the trial and judgment? How many persons are required for a jury in a justice's court? State how jury trials are conducted. In case the jury fail to agree, what is done? How are jurors procured in justices' courts? What is said of an execution? Of the stay of execution? Of the removal of the cause to the court of common pleas? What is said of property exempt from levy and sale on execution?

MILITARY DEPARTMENT.

CHAPTER XLIII.

THE STATE MILITIA—WHO LIABLE TO PERFORM MILITARY DUTY —INDEPENDENT MILITIA.

Able-bodied white male citizens between the ages of eighteen and forty-five years, are, unless exempt by law, subject to military duty.

The officers acting as assessors in the several townships, precincts and wards, are required to return to the county auditors two lists of persons liable to military duty. One list to embrace those who are exempt from service in the militia, except in case of war, insurrection, invasion, or the reasonable apprehension thereof, namely: those who have served in the army or navy of the United States one year during the late rebellion and have been honorably discharged; all who have served five years in the militia; all who served in the one hundred days service under the call of the governor in 1864; and active members of volunteer fire companies. Those who have served for five consecutive years in any regularly organized fire company, are for five years thereafter exempt from military service in time of peace, and from labor on the highways. The other list to embrace all others subject to enrollment.

The persons exempt from military duty are those engaged in the United States service or are exempt by the laws of the United States; those unfit for service by reason of permanent physical disability idiots, lunatics, and felons convicted of infamous crimes unless pardoned; all members of religious denominations whose articles of faith prohibit them from performing military duty.

The county auditors are required to transmit a statement showing the number of each class enrolled in each township or ward to the adjutant general of the State. The law provides that the organized militia of the State shall be composed of such volunteer companies as were organized or retained under the militia acts of April 14, 1863 and March 31, 1864, and are not discharged by the governor, and such further companies as may be formed under the act of April 2, 1866.

The law of 1866 provides that the governor may authorize the formation of such number of volunteer companies of infantry, artillery and cavalry as the good of the service may indicate.

In case of riot, mob, etc., the State troops may be called to aid the civil authorities.

In case of war, invasion, insurrection, the reasonable apprehension of invasion or insurrection, riot, or any forcible obstruction to the execution of the laws, the governor may not only call out the militia, but may either call for volunteer recruits or authorize the organization of other volunteer companies, or both.

When the volunteer and organized militia are insufficient, the governor may order a draft.

The governor is commander-in chief of the military forces of the State, and is required to appoint an adjutant-general who shall rank as brigadier-general.

In case of war, invasion, or insurrection, a commissary and medical department may be organized.

Field officers of regiments and battalions are elected by ballot by the members of the respective regiments or battalions; commissioned officers of the line, by the members of their respective companies. Adjutants, quartermasters, chaplains, surgeons, surgeons mates, sergeant-majors, quartermaster-sergeants, commissary-sergeants, drum-majors, and fife-majors, are appointed by the respective commanding officers of regiments.

Sergeant-majors and quartermaster-sergeants of battalions are appointed by the commanding officers thereof. Non-commissioned officers of companies are appointed by the respective commandants of companies.

The military officers of the State, whether elected or appointed are commissioned by the governor.

In 1870, a law was passed authorizing the enrolled militia in counties having cities or towns with a larger population than three thousand, to organize themselves into independent companies, battallions, squadrons, regiments and batteries, to be subject solely to the direct call of the governor of the State, and of the regular constituted civil authorities, for the suppression of insurrection and riot, or the repelling of invasion or the enforcement of the execution of the laws. These independent companies are entitled to the use of the public arms of the State. Nearly every one, if not all of the present military organizations of the State, are organized under the "Independent Militia Law" of 1870.

Questions—What persons are subject to military duty? What are the assessors required to do with reference to making lists of persons liable to military duty? What persons are to be embraced in each of the two lists? What persons are exempt from military duty? What statements are the county auditors required to furnish to the adjutant-general of the State? What constitutes the organized militia of the State? What is said of the law of 1866? In what cases may the State troops be required to aid the civil authorities? When may the governor call out the militia? What else may he do with reference to raising troops? What is the official relation of the governor to the military forces of the State? What military officer is he required to appoint? When may a medical and a commissary department be organized? How are field officers of the line elected? Commissioned officers of the line? What officers are appointed by the commanding officers of regiments? Of battalions? Of companies? What is said of the law of 1870, and of the independent military organizations?

10

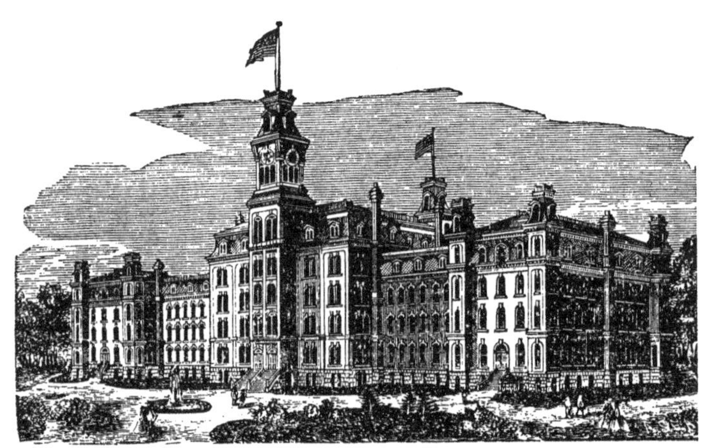

UNIVERSITY OF WOOSTER, O

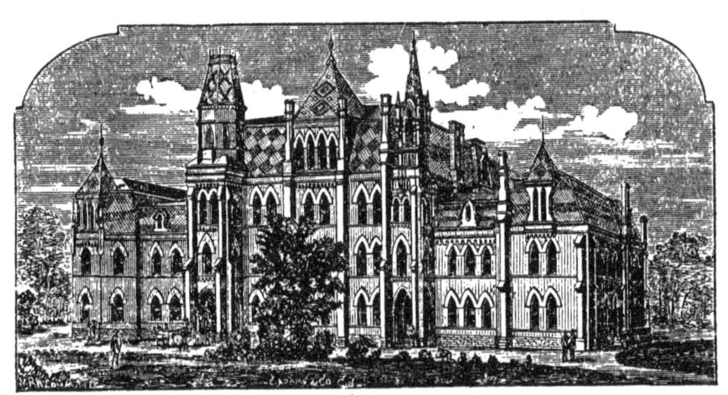

OTTERBIEN UNIVERSITY, AT WESTERVILLE, O.

EDUCATION AND EDUCATIONAL INSTITUTIONS.

CHAPTER XLIV.

COMMON SCHOOLS—CLASSIFICATION OF DISTRICTS—BOARDS OF EDUCATION — COMMISSIONER OF COMMON SCHOOLS — EXAMINERS OF TEACHERS—QUALIFICATIONS OF TEACHERS.

We have seen, in a preceding chapter, that those who participated in the organization of government in the Northwest Territory, recognized religion, morality, and knowledge, as necessary to good government and the happiness of mankind. We have also seen that under the State government, as early as 1825, a uniform school system was established.

Under the present law, the State is divided into school districts, as follows:

City districts of the first class, city districts of the second class, village districts, special districts, and township districts.

To administer the affairs of the districts, and to look

after and promote the educational interests therein, the law has provided for the establishment of boards of education in each district. These boards may acquire real or personal property for the use of their districts, and are required to establish schools for the free education of the youth of school age, and may establish schools of a higher grade than the primary schools. They are to determine the studies to be pursued and the text-books to be used in the schools under their control; to appoint superintendents of schools, teachers and other employees, and fix their salaries. They are authorized to make such rules and regulations as they may deem expedient and necessary for the government of the board, their appointees, and pupils.

The following provisions are made by law in regard to the establishment of schools and the studies to be persued therein:

"Each board of education shall establish a sufficient number of schools to provide for the free education of the youth of school age within the district, at such places as will be most convenient for the attendance of the largest number of such youth, and also may establish one or more schools of higher grade than the primary schools whenever they deem the establishment of such school or schools proper or necessary for the convenience or progress in studies of the pupils attending the same, or for the conduct and welfare of the educational interests of such district; and the board shall continue each and every day school established by them for not less than twenty-four nor more than forty-four weeks in each school year; provided, that each township board of education shall establish at least one primary school in each sub-district of their township; and the boards of education of the districts in which a "Children's Home" is or may be established under an act entitled "an act for the establishment, support and regulation of Children's Homes in the several counties of the State," etc. passed April 7, 1867, and in districts in which a county infirmary is or may be located, when requested by the board of trustees of such "Children's Home," or the directors of such county infirmary, are hereby authorized and required to establish in such home or infirmary a separate school so as to afford to the children therein so far as practicable the advantages and privileges of a common school education; and such school shall be continued in operation each year until the full share of all the school funds of the township or district belonging to said children on the basis of the enumeration shall have been expended; and all schools so established shall be under the control and management of the board of education or other school officers who have charge of the common schools of such district: Provided, that in the establishment of said schools the county commissioners of the county in which such "Children's Home" or county infirmary may be established, shall provide the necessary school room or rooms, furniture, apparatus and books, which they are hereby empowered to do; and provided further, that such boards of education shall incur no expense in supporting said schools, except in the payment of the teachers.

" In any district composed, in whole or in part, of any city or incorporated village, the board of education may, at their discretion, provide a suitable number of evening schools for the instruction of such youth as are prevented by their daily vocation from attending day schools, subject to such regulations as said board from time to time may adopt for the government thereof.

" Each board of education shall determine the studies to be pursued and the text books to be used in the schools under their control, and no text book shall be changed within three years after its adoption, without the consent of three-fourths of the members of the board of education, given at a regular meeting; and it shall be the duty of the boards of education to cause the German language to be taught in any of the public schools of this State when demanded by seventy-five freeholders residents of said school district, representing not less than forty pupils, who shall in good faith desire and intend to study the German and English languages together: Provided, that nothing herein contained shall be construed as preventing said boards of education from causing the German or other languages to be taught in said schools; and provided further, that all branches taught in the common schools of this State shall be in the English language."

A State commissioner of common schools is elected by the people, whose term of office continues for three years. He is required to superintend and encourage teacher's institutes, confer with boards of education or other school officers, counsel teachers, visit schools, and deliver lectures calculated to promote popular education. He is to have a supervision over the school funds, and has power by law to require proper returns to be made by the officers who have duties to perform pertaining to schools or school funds. It is his duty to give instructions for the organization and government of schools, and to distribute the school laws and other documents for the use of school officers.

The State commissioner of common schools is required by law to appoint a board of State examiners, consisting of three persons, who hold their office for two years. This board is authorized to issue life certificates to such teachers as may be found, upon examination, to have attained "eminent professional experience and ability." These certificates are valid in any school district in the State, and supersede the necessity of all other examinations by the county or local boards of examiners.

Each applicant for a State certificate is required to pay a fee of three dollars.

Each county has a board of examiners appointed by

the probate judge. Their term of office continues for three years.

The law provides that "it shall be the duty of the examiners to fix upon the time of holding the meetings for the examination of teachers, in such places in their respective counties as will, in their opinion, best accommodate the greatest number of candidates for examination, notice of all such meetings being published in some newspaper of general circulation in their respective counties; and at such meetings any two of said board shall be competent to examine applicants and grant certificates: and as a condition of examination, each applicant for a certificate shall pay the board of examiners a fee of fifty cents."

The fees thus received are set apart as a fund for the support of teacher's institutes.

In city districts of the first and second class, and village districts having a population of not less than twenty-five hundred, the examiners are appointed by the boards of education.

The fees received for these examinations—fifty cents for each application—are appropriated for the support of teachers' institutes.

The certificates granted by the county examiners are not valid in those districts where the examiners are appointed by the board of education, unless endorsed by the president and secretary of the boards of examiners of such districts; and certificates granted by city district examiners are valid only in the districts where granted.

Certificates granted by county examiners are valid only for six, twelve, eighteen, or twenty-four months, and those granted by district boards are valid only for ~~either~~ one, two, or three years.

The law provides that "no person shall be employed as a teacher in any common school, unless such person shall have first obtained from a board of examiners having competent jurisdiction, or a majority of them, a certificate of good moral character, and that he or she is qualified to teach orthography, reading, writing, arithmetic, geography, English grammar, and posesses an adequate knowledge of the theory and practice of teaching; and in case such person be required to teach other branches than those herein specified, he or she shall first obtain a certificate of the requisite qualifications, in addition to the branches aforesaid."

Boards of examiners have power to revoke certificates, on good cause shown.

Questions—Name the classes of school districts into which the State is divided. For what purposes are boards of education established? Enumerate their powers and duties. What number of schools are the boards of education required to establish? What provision is made with reference to the establishment of graded schools? How long must day schools be continued in each school year? What is said in relation to "Children's Home" and county infirmary? Of evening schools? Of studies and text books? Of the German and other languages? What is said of the election, duties, and powers of the State commissioner of common schools? Of the appointment of State examiners, and their duties? What provision is made by law for the appointment of county examiners? What are their powers and duties? In what districts are the examiners appointed by the boards of education? What is said as to the validity of the certificates granted by the different boards? What is said of the qualifications of teachers?

CHAPTER XLV.

COMMON SCHOOLS—SUB-DISTRICTS—LOCAL DIRECTORS—TOWNSHIP BOARD OF EDUCATION—ENUMERATION OF YOUTH—APPORTIONMENT OF SCHOOL FUNDS—SCHOOL YEAR, SCHOOL WEEK AND SCHOOL MONTH—WHO MAY ATTEND COMMON SCHOOLS—SUSPENSION AND EXPULSION OF PUPILS.

There are in the different townships, sub-districts, in which the people elect, annually, a local director, whose term of office continues for three years. From this it will be seen that each sub-district has a board consisting of three directors. These directors choose one of their number as clerk, who presides at the meetings of the local directors, and keeps a record thereof. He also keeps a record of the proceedings of the annual school meetings of the sub-district.

The board of education of each township district consists of the township clerk and the local directors, who have been appointed clerks of the sub-districts.

The law provides that "in every district in the State, there shall be taken, between the first Monday in September and the first Monday in October, in each year, an enumeration of all unmarried youth, noting race and sex, between six and twenty-one years of age, resident within the district, and not temporarily there, designating also the number between sixteen and twenty-one years of age, the number residing in the Western Reserve, the Virginia Military District, the United States Military District, and in any original surveyed township or fractional township to which belongs section sixteen, or other land in lieu thereof, or any other lands for the use of schools or any interest in the proceeds of such land: Provided, that in addition to the classified return of all the youth residing in the district, that the aggregate number of youth in the district resident of any adjoining county shall be seperately given, if any such there be, and the name of the county in which they reside."

In a township district, this enumeration must be taken, or caused to be taken, in the sub-districts by the local directors who have been elected clerks, between the first and third Mondays of September, and a certified copy thereof returned to the township clerk. The enumeration in joint sub-districts must be returned to the clerk of the township in which the school-house is situated; the number of youth, male and female, residing in the respective parts of the several townships being designated in the return. In all other districts, the enumeration is required to be taken between the first Monday in September and the first Monday in October. In addition to the classified return of all the unmarried youth of school age residing in the district, those in the district who are residents of an adjoining county should be separately given, and the name of the county in which they reside.

The clerk of each district other than a township district, is required to employ one or more competent persons to take and return this enumeration.

The clerk of each board of education is required to transmit to the county auditor an abstract of the returns of enumeration made to him, on or before the second Monday of October.

The county audtitor is required to transmit to the State commissioner, on or before the fifth day of November, a duly certified abstract of the enumeration returns made to him by clerks of school districts.*

The law provides that "the auditor of state shall, annually, apportion the common school funds among the different counties upon the enumeration and returns made to him by the State commissoner of common schools, and certify the amount so apportioned to the county auditor of each county, stating from what sources the same is derived, which said sum the several county treasurers shall retain in their respective treasuries from the State funds; and the county auditors shall, annually, and immediately after their annual settlement with the county treasurers, apportion the school funds for their respective counties according to the enumeration and returns in their respective offices."

The law provides that the school year shall begin on the first day of September of each year, and close on the thirty-first day of August of the succeeding year.

A school week shall consist of five days, a school month of four school weeks.

The law provides in relation to our common schools that they shall be "free to all youth between six and twenty-one years of age who are children, wards or apprentices of actual residents of the school district and no pupil shall be suspended therefrom except for such time as may be necessary to convene the board of education of the district, or local directors of the sub-district, nor be expelled unless by a vote of two-thirds of said board of local directors, after the parent or guardian of the offending pupil shall have been notified of the proposed expulsion, and permitted to be heard against the same; and no scholar shall be suspended or expelled from the privilege of schools beyond the current term: Provided, that each board of education shall have power to admit other persons, not under six years of age, upon such terms or upon

* From the Report of the State Commissioner of Common Schools, for 1873.

the payment of such tuition as they prescribe; and boards of education of city, village or special districts shall also have power to admit, without charge for tuition, persons within the school age who are members of the family of any freeholder whose residence is not within such district, if any part of such freeholder's homestead is within such district; and, provided further, that the several boards of education shall make such assignment of the youth of their respective districts, to the schools established by them as will, in their opinion, best promote the interests of education in their districts; and provided further that nothing contained in in this section shall supersede or modify the provisions of section thirty-one of an act entitled an act for the reorganization, supervision and maintenance of common schools, passed March 14, 1853, as amended March 18, 1864. [The amended section relates to colored children—See Swan and Sayler, 705.]

"All property, real or personal, vested in any board of education, shall be exempted from tax and from sale on any execution or other writ or order in the nature of an execution."

Questions—What is said with reference to sub-districts and directors? Of the clerk? Of what officers does the township board of education consist? What is said of the annual enumeration of certain persons? By whom, to whom, and for what purpose are abstracts of the ennmeration sent? What is required of the auditor-general with reference to the enumeration? What is a school year? A school week? A school month? Who may attend the schools, and on what conditions? What is said with reference to the suspension and expulsion of pupils? What is said of the taxing of school property?

CHAPTER XLVI.

TEACHERS' INSTITUTES—CERTAIN RIGHTS AND PRIVILEGES OF TEACHERS — SCHOOL FUNDS — SCHOOL STATISTICS FOR 1874.

Provision is made by law for the establishment and maintenance of teachers' institutes.

The institutes are established for the professional improvement of teachers. At each session competent instructors and lecturers are employed to assist the State commissioner, who is required by law to superintend and encourage such institutes.

These institutes are either county institutes, city institutes, or joint institutes of two or more counties.

The examination fees paid by teachers to examiners are devoted to the payment of the expenses of the intutes.

The following provision is made by law, in relation to city institutes and joint institutes of two or more counties:

"The board of education of any city district of the first class are authorized to provide for holding yearly an institute for the improvement of the teachers of the schools under their control, which institute shall continue not less than four days, and the board are hereby authorized in defraying the expenses of such institute to use the city institute fund arising from the examination fees of teachers, or any other moneys under their control; provided, that if said board shall not hold one institute in any school year, that said board shall cause an order to be issued on the treasurer in favor of the county treasurer for such institute fund, which the county treasurer shall place to the credit of the county fund, in which case the teachers of such city districts shall be entitled to the advantages of the county institute.

Whenever a teachers' association, formed for the professional improvement of the teachers of several adjacent counties, shall organize a teachers' institute for the specific purpose of providing for the professional instruction of the teachers of the graded schools in such adjacent counties, any and all boards of education of city districts of the first and second class, village districts and special districts within said counties shall have power to contribute to such institutes from the institute and other funds under their control, and to permit the teachers employed by them to attend the same for one week without forfeiture of wages."

Each teacher employed in the common schools has a right to dismiss his or her school, without forfeiture of pay, on New Years's day, the Fourth of July, Christmas, and on any day set apart by proclamation of the President of the United States, or the governor of Ohio, as a thanksgiving or fast day.

Any teacher in any public school is authorized to dismiss the school for the week in which is held the county teachers' institute, for the purpose of attending the same, and such teacher shall not thereby forfeit his or her pay for such week; provided such teacher shall deposit with the clerk of the board a certifiate from the secretary of the institute that he or she has been present at such institute for not less than four days; provided, that this privilege is not extended to teachers in city districts of the first class, without the consent of the board of education thereof, and that no union or graded school shall be dismissed except when a majority of the teachers in such school are in favor of such dismission.

The following in relation to school funds, school lands, etc., is from the report of of the State commissioner of common schools, for the year 1873:

"The State common school fund consists of such sum as will be produced by the annual levy and assessment of one mill upon the dollar valuation, on the grand list of the taxable property of the State. In addition to this fund, the moneys arising from the sale of lands appropriated by Congress for the support of schools, constitute an irreducible fund, the proceeds accruing from which are distributed to the proper districts to be used for school purposes.

"The irreducible school funds are: (1) The *Virginia Military School Fund*, the proceeds of the sale of lands selected from Congress lands lying between the United States Military Tract and the Connecticut Western Reserve—equivalent to one thirty-sixth part of the Virginia Military Reservation. (2) The *United States Military School Fund*, the proceeds of the sale of lands selected in the United States Military District, and equivalent in quantity to one thirty-sixth part of the area of that reservation. (3) The *Western Reserve School Fund*, the proceeds of the sale of lands situated in the United States Military District, and of lands in Defiance, Williams, Paulding, Putnam, and VanWert counties, appropriated for the use of schools in the Connecticut Western Reserve, and equivalent to one thirty-sixth part of that district. (4) *Section Sixteen*, the proceeds of one thirty-sixth part of each township—the sixteenth section—in which the Indian title was not extinguished in 1803. (5) The *Moravian School Fund*, the proceeds of the sale of one thirty-sixth part of each of three tracts of four thousand acres each situated in Tuscarawas county. (6) The *Ohio University Fund*, the proceeds of the sale of a part of the land granted by Congress for the purpose of endowing the Ohio University. (7) The *Ohio Agricultural and Mechanical*

College Fund, the proceeds of the sale of 629,920 acres of land granted by Congress as an endowment for that college.

"The Virginia Military District includes the whole of Adams, Brown, Clermont, Clinton, Fayette, Highland, Madison, and Union counties; one-half of Hardin, Franklin, and Logan; one-fourth of Champaign county, one-sixth of Clarke, three-fourths of Greene, two-fifths of Warren and Scioto, three-fifths of Pike, two-thirds of Ross and Pickaway, one-fifth of Delaware and Marion, Anderson township in Hamilton county, and part of Goshen township in Auglaize county.

"The United States Military District includes all of Coshocton county, the greater part of Licking, Knox, Delaware, Tuscarawas, and Guernsey, about one-half of Morrow and Muskingum, two-thirds of Holmes, one-third of Franklin, parts of two townships in Marion, and one quarter township in Noble county.

"The Connecticut Western Reserve includes all of Ashtabula, Trumbull, Lake, Geauga, Portage, Cuyahoga, Medina, Lorain, Huron, and Erie counties, all of Summit county excepting two townships, one-half of Mahoning, three townships in Ashland, and Danbury township in Ottawa county."

The following is a summary of the school statistics of Ohio for the year ending August 31, 1874, as appears by the report of the secretary of state:

Number of primary schools	14,356
" high schools	412
" teachers in primary schools	21,664
" teachers in high schools	711
" scholars enrolled in primary schools	683,644
" scholars enrolled in high schools	24,299
Amount paid teachers in primary schools	$4,196,408 20
" " high schools	408,101 25
" for sites and buildings	1,472,100 95
" for fuel and other contingent expenses	1,328,462 00
" on bonds and interest	516,603 20
Making the total amount paid	8,072,167 65

Total enumeration of youth, six to twenty-one years of age	988,180
Average amount paid for school purposes for each youth enumerated	$8 16
Number of universities and colleges	36
Number of academies, normal schools, etc	44
Number of schools of theology	12
" " law	3
" " medicine	11

Questions—What is said of the establishment of teachers' institutes? How are they maintained? What is said of city institutes? Of joint institutes of two or more counties? With reference to certain days on which teachers of common schools need not teach? With reference to the attendance of teachers at teachers' institutes? What is said, in this connection, in relation to teachers in districts of the first class? Of teachers in union or graded schools? What *per cent.* on the valuation of the property of the State is levied for the use of common schools? From what other sources are moneys derived for the support of schools? Of the "irreducible school funds," mention the first as given in the lesson, and state what is said in relation thereto. The second. Third. Fourth. Fifth. Sixth. Seventh. What territory is embraced within the Virginia military district? U. S. military district? The Connecticut Western Reserve? How many primary schools were there in Ohio in 1874? High schools? Teachers in primary schools? Teachers in high schools? Scholars enrolled in primary schools? In high schools? Amount paid teachers in primary schools? In high schools? For sites and buildings? For fuel and other contingent expenses? On bonds and interest? Total amount paid? What was the total enumeration of youth between six and twenty-one years of age? Average amount paid for all school purposes for each youth enumerated? Number of universities and colleges? Number of academies, normal schools, etc.? Of schools of theology? Law? Medicine?

CHAPTER XLVII.

UNIVERSITIES, COLLEGES, NORMAL SCHOOLS, FEMALE SEMINARIES AND ACADEMIES.

CIN. WESLEYAN COL. FOR YOUNG LADIES.

A universal school, or *university*, is one in which all the most important branches of science are taught, and which has, at the same time, the right to confer honorary distinctions on scientific merit.

A full university course embraces theology, medicine, law, and the sciences and arts.

The word *university* was used in France during the period of the empire to designate the collective body of the highest institutions of education, consisting of twenty-six academies in the principal cities, all under the control of a common head.

"The several *faculties* of a university are subordinate corporations, consisting of the aggregate of students or teachers in a praticular department of knowledge. The number of faculties has varied much in different universities. The University of Paris had at first only a faculty of arts, which, as early as 1169, existed as a separate body, with an organization of its own. Faculties of theology, medicine, and cannon law were added in the thirteenth century."*

The word *college*, in its primary sense, signifies a collection or assembly. This name is also given to a society of persons engaged in the pursuits of literature. These institutions, like universities, are incorporated or established by the legislative power of the State.

Originally, colleges were members of a university, and had no power to confer degrees. But in America and in Scotland this distinction is lost sight of, and colleges and universities alike confer degrees.

Normal Schools are established for the instruction and training of teachers in their profession. In England they are called Training Colleges and in Germany Seminaries. The first normal school established in Great Britian was the Sessional School of Edinburg, in 1830. The first one established in America was in 1839, at Lexington, in Massachusetts. In 1870 there were eighty-two normal schools in America.

Though most of these schools are supported by individual enterprise, a number of them are supported by the States in which they are located.

The educators of this State are by no means agreed touching the policy that should be pursued in relation to the normal schools. Some believe the State should encourage them by furnishing material aid; while others not only question the propriety of such support, but believe that they are "antagonistic in aim and purpose" to our free high schools.

---

*Chambers's Encyclopedia.

THE NORTHWESTERN OHIO NORMAL SCHOOL AT ADA.

These differences of opinion will induce discussion and investigation, and in this way the people will be prepared to judge wisely concerning the merits of these schools, and pursue such a course in relation to them as shall tend to promote the cause of education.

In common acceptation, the word *academy* is applied to institutions of learning of a grade between common schools and colleges. Strictly speaking, however, it signifies "a society of savans or artists established for the promotion of literature, science or art."

Speaking of the female seminaries, the late State commissioner of common schools, in his report for 1873, says:

"Our female seminaries have ceased to be schools in which 'accomplishments' only are taught. Their courses of study rarely differ in any essential particular from those of our high schools and academies for boys. * * They are doing a good work, and the friends of education should take a lively interest in their welfare."

Questions—What is a university? What does a full university course embrace? What did the word *university* signify in France during the period of the empire? What is said of the faculties of a university? Of the University of Paris? What does the word *college* signify? How are colleges established? What is said of the relation of colleges to universities, originally? Of degrees? Does this distinction continue? For what purpose are normal schools established? What are they called in England? In Germany? When and where was the first normal school established in Great Britain? In America? How many normal schools were there in America in 1870? What is said of their support? What is said of academies? Of female seminaries?

UNIVERSITIES, COLLEGES, NORMAL SCHOOLS AND SEMINARIES OF OHIO.

[The information embraced in the following table in relation to the institutions marked with a star, (*) is derived from the report of the State commissioner of common schools, for the year 1873. The figures relating to those

---

There are several medical colleges and other educational institutions in the State, not embraced in this table, as the author was unable to procure any reliable information concerning them, in time for insertion in this work.

marked with a dagger (†), are taken from the report of the secretary of state, for the year 1873. All the rest have been furnished by the presidents and principals of the several institutions to which they refer, and show the condition of such schools for the year 1874.

The author had intended to give a brief history of the several universities, colleges, etc., of the State, but has been compelled to abandon that purpose, in order to give room for other matter deemed more essential.]

Name of Institution.	Location.	Date of charter or organization.	No. Stud'ts Total.	Males.	Females.	No. of Instructors	Total cash value of property.	Total No. of volumes in libraries.
Antioch College	Yellow Springs	1852	99	49	50	9	$200,000	5.000
*Atwood Institute	Athens	----	235	110	125	3	12,000	----
Baldwin University	Berea	1846	288	158	130	10	180,000	2,000
†Bloomingburg Academy	Bloomingburg	1864	144	----	----	--	--------	----
Buchtel College	Akron	1869	188	99	89	12	275,000	1,000
*Capital University	Columbus	1850	72	72	----	6	--------	3,000
Cin. Col. of Med'n and Surg'y	Cincinnati	----	----	----	----	--	--------	----
Cin. Wesleyan Col for Ladies	Cincinnati	1842	220	----	220	18	225,000	1,000
Clermont Academy	New Richmond	1839	105	71	34	2	3,000	1,000
Cleveland Female Sem	Cleveland	1853	124	----	124	12	200,000	2,000
Cleveland Medical College	Cleveland	1845	----	----	----	--	--------	----
Cleveland Academy	Cleveland	1864	140	70	70	10	20,000	50
†Columbus Business College	Columbus	1865	220	----	----	--	--------	----
*Cooper Seminary	Dayton	1845	145	----	----	8	--------	1,300
Denison University	Granville	1831	168	168	----	10	275,000	11,000
Eclectic Medical Institute	Cincinnati	1845	207	207	----	7	60,000	----
†Ellis' Academy	Cincinnati	----	41	----	----	--	--------	----
†Euclid Avenue Branch Sem	Cleveland	1869	55	----	----	--	--------	----
†Ewington Academy	Ewington	1857	90	----	----	--	--------	----
†Franklin Business Institute	Columbus	1870	170	----	----	--	--------	----
Franklin College	New Athens	1825	100	----	----	4	--------	----
*Friends' Boarding School	Mt. Pleasant	1837	74	34	40	6	15,000	2,000
Gallia Academy	Gallipolis	1811	130	75	55	3	25,000	250
German Wallace College	Berea	1864	110	89	21	11	83,000	700
Glendale Female College	Glendale	1854	123	----	123	12	75,000	2,300
Grand River Institute	Austinburg	1831	326	170	156	6	--------	1,500
Granville Female College	Granville	1836	125	----	125	12	--------	----
*Greenway Boarding School	Springfield	1848	10	10	----	--	18,000	250
Heidelberg College	Tiffin	1850	196	155	41	6	125,000	4,000
*Highland Institute	Hillsborough	1857	55	----	55	7	100,000	2,000
Hillsborough Fem. College	Hillsborough	1856	70	----	70	6	40,000	800
Hiram College	Hiram	1850	235	116	119	9	--------	2,000
Homœpathic Medical Col	Cleveland	----	----	----	----	--	--------	----
Hudson Ladies Seminary	Hudson	1844	38	----	38	2	2,000	40
Kenyon College	Gambier	1824	65	65	----	7	250,000	19,000
Lake Erie Female Seminary	Painesville	1859	123	----	123	11	110,000	1,450
Marietta College	Marietta	1835	183	183	----	9	200,000	26,000
Medical College of Ohio	Cincinnati	1819	280	280	----	10	--------	2,000
Miami Medical	Cincinnati	1852	127	----	----	11	40,000	----
*McCorkle Medical College	Bloomfield	1873	32	21	11	3	16,400	75

(TABLE OF UNIVERSITIES, COLLEGES, &c., CONTINUED.)

Name of Institution.	Location.	Date of charter or organization.	No. Stud'ts Total.	No. Stud'ts Males.	No. Stud'ts Females.	No. of Instructors	Total cash value of property.	Total No. of volumes in libraries.
*McNeely's Normal School	Hopedale	1855	133	74	59	5	47,000	2,000
*Mount Union College	Mount Union	1846	832	598	234	16	413,625	3,675
Mount Auburn Ladies Inst.	Cincinnati	1856	121	----	121	15	125,000	1,000
Mt. St. Mary's Seminary	Cincinnati	----	110	110	----	16	170,000	14,800
†Morning Sun Academy	Morning Sun	1852	47	----	----	--	--------	- ----
Muskingum College	New Concord	1837	110	78	32	3	25,000	500
National Normal School	Lebanon	1855	1657	1333	324	17	90,000	3,500
New Hagerstown Academy	N'w Hagerstown	1837	81	44	37	2	1,300	- ----
Northwestern Normal Sch'l	Fostoria	1870	400	250	150	6	15,000	2,000
Notre Dame Academy	Cincinnati	1843	200	----	200	14	--------	3,000
Oberlin College	Oberlin	1834	1336	701	635	26	530,000	12,000
Ohio Ag'l & Mech'l College	Columbus	1870	50	44	6	9	1,000,000	1,000
*Ohio Central College	Iberia	1854	116	83	33	4	15,000	647
Ohio University	Athens	1804	105	95	10	6	190,000	8,000
Ohio Wesleyan University	Delaware	1845	374	374	----	10	375,000	10,000
Ohio Wesl'n Female College	Delaware	1853	217	----	217	10	120,000	1,500
†Ohio Female College	College Hill	1848	27	----	27	--	--------	- ----
Ohio Central Normal School	Worthington	1871	215	105	110	3	15,000	600
One Study University	Scio	1866	204	130	74	4	30,000	1,000
Orwell Normal Institute	Orwell	1852	192	100	92	3	6,000	300
Otterbein University	Westerville	1847	266	176	90	6	100,000	1,200
Oxford Female College	Oxford	1854	120	----	120	9	100,000	2,000
*Pierpont Academy	Pierpont	1868	147	----	----	--	--------	- ----
Poland Union Seminary	Poland	1862	164	81	83	4	30,000	350
*Portsmouth Seminary	Portsmouth	1867	77	20	57	4	33,000	100
Putnam Female Seminary	Zanesville	1838	88	----	88	8	42,000	2,500
Richmond College	Richmond	1835	121	80	41	4	25,000	- ----
*Saint Xavier College	Cincinnati	1842	304	304	----	13	150,000	16,000
St. Mary's Inst. Nazereth	Dayton	1850	240	240	[illegible]	13	120,000	400
Savannah Academy	Savannah	1859	200	100	100	3	16,000	1,000
Smithville High School	Smithville	1865	325	200	125	5	20,000	600
Starr's Institute	Seven Mile	1861	12	12	----	2	3,500	100
Sterling Medical College	Columbus	----	----	----	----	--	--------	- ----
Steubenville Female Sem'y	Steubenville	1829	175	----	175	16	40,000	3,000
University of Wooster	Wooster	1868	220	178	42	10	350,000	- ----
*Urbana University	Urbana	1850	26	26	----	4	35,000	5,000
Van Sickles' Business Col	Springfield	1871	45	35	10	1	125	- ----
Western Female Seminary	Oxford	1853	154	----	154	14	--------	1,620
Western Reserve College	Hudson	1826	123	118	5	9	300,000	10,000
Western Res. Medical Col	Hudson	1826	----	----	----	--	--------	- ----
Western Reserve Seminary	W. Farmington	1855	133	64	69	4	35,000	- ----
*West'rn Res. Normal Inst.	Milan	1832	133	68	65	4	5,000	- ----
*Westminister Academy	Waterford	1869	73	50	23	5	3,500	1,200
Wilberforce University	Xenia	1863	156	85	40	5	62,000	3,500
Willoughby College	Willoughby	1859	150	75	75	5	50,000	- ----
Wilmington College	Wilmington	1871	80	38	42	4	50,000	500
Wittenburg College	Springfield	1845	140	140	----	9	100,000	7,000
Xenia College	Xenia	1850	271	101	170	7	25,000	300

The Hand Performs the Office of the Tongue.

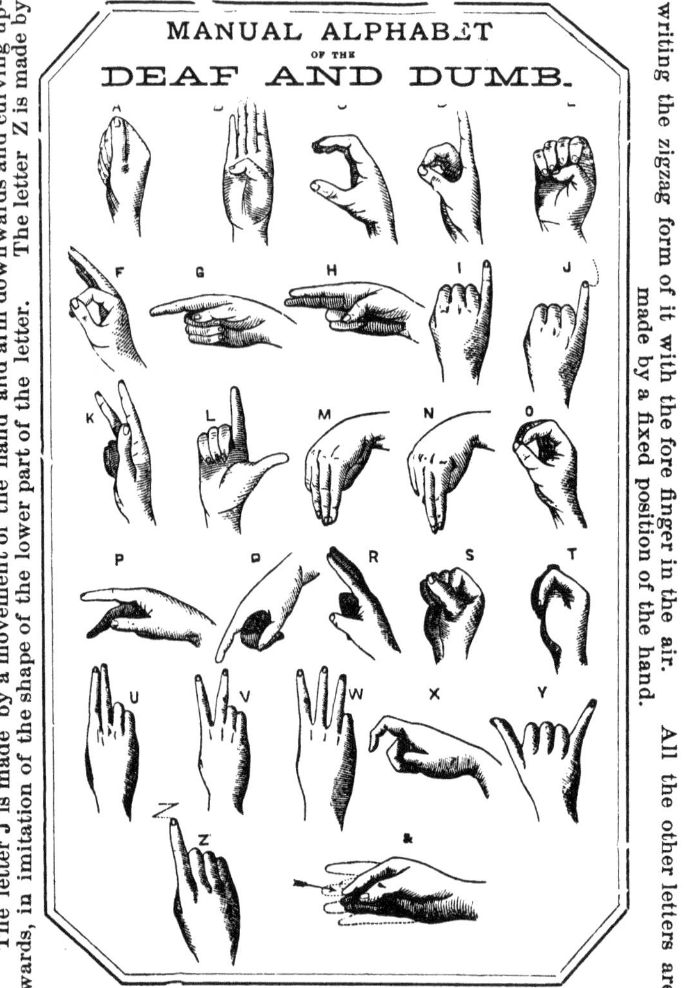

The letter J is made by a movement of the hand and arm downwards and curving upwards, in imitation of the shape of the lower part of the letter. The letter Z is made by writing the zigzag form of it with the fore finger in the air. All the other letters are made by a fixed position of the hand.

Earth speaks With many Tongues, Heaven knows but One.

BENEVOLENT, PENAL AND REFORMATORY INSTITUTIONS.

CHAPTER XLVIII.

BENEVOLENT INSTITUTIONS.

Such institutions as are supported by the State, or some subdivision thereof, as a county, city, village or township, are called public institutions, while those supported by private charities, or from means other than public revenue, are called private institutions.

The Ohio Institution for the Education of Deaf-Mutes, at Columbus.—This, the oldest of the so-called benevolent institutions of the State, was established in 1827. Instruction is given in all the branches usually taught in the public schools. Attention is devoted chiefly to the aquisition of the ability to read and write the English language correctly. In promising cases instruction is also given in the arts of articulation and lip reading. A part of the day is spent in manual labor, the boys thereby acquiring a knowledge of a mechanical trade.

The institution is open, free of charge, to all deaf mutes of a sound intellect, who are between the ages of six and twenty-one, and are residents of the State. Their time is limited to ten years. The average time spent by mutes at the institute is less than five years.

Ohio State Asylum for the Education of Feeble-Minded and Imbecile Youth, located at Columbus, was established in 1857, by the General Assembly of the State. After a successful trial of several years with a small number of pupils, the General Assembly appropriated generously, and in 1868 it moved to its present healthful location and commodious buildings on the bluffs, two miles from the city. Its object is to furnish special means of improvement to those children who are deficient, or have such peculiarities of intellect as to deprive them of other methods of instruction. The education given includes not only the similar studies of our common schools, so far as that is possible, but embraces a course of training in the more practical matters of every day life—the cultivation of habits of cleanliness, propriety, self-management, self-reliance, and the development of a capacity for useful occupation.

Ohio Institution for the Education of the Blind, at Columbus, was opened in 1837, and is supported by the State.

Applicants between the ages of six and twenty-one years are admitted, and allowed to attend such portion of the time until they are twenty-one as their abilities and improvement seem, in the judgment of the trustees and superintendent, to warrant.

Persons of good habits, over twenty-one years of age, are admitted to learn a trade.

For residents of the State the school is free, no charge being made for board or tution; but parents and guardians must provide their children with ~~good and~~ suitable clothing, and pay their traveling expenses, and should also deposite with the steward a small sum for occasional expenses. For pupils residing out of the State, the terms are one hundred and twenty dollars per annum, payable half yearly in advance.

The institution is not an asylum to which the blind are brought merely to be kept, but a school for educating them in morals, science, music, employments, and all that pertains to manhood and womanhood.

The Northwestern Hospital for the Insane, near Toledo, was organized by the present superintendent, B. A. Wright, M. D., December 1st, 1871. It has a district embracing seven counties, viz.: Lucas, Ottawa, Wood, Fulton, Williams, Henry and Defiance.

The buildings belong to Lucas county. A daily average of 100 patients ~~are~~ maintained by the State at a yearly cost of $25,028. 27.

The Western Ohio Hospital for the Insane, located at Dayton, where, in 1852, fifty acres of land were donated for it, was first opened in 1855. Since then the State has purchased for its use one hundred and seven acres ~~more~~ of land, at a cost of $23,455, 62.

Since its organization 3,564 insane persons have been admitted and treated, of whom 1,650 have recovered. The present number of inmates (December 30th, 1874) is 540.

The institution is supported by the State at an annual

cost of about $100,000, and is under the control of a board of trustees appointed by the governor.

For the management of the institution the trustees appoint a medical superintendent, two assistant physicians, a steward and a matron. About seventy-five attendants and employes are required in and about the hospital.

The hospital grounds and farm contain about 170 acres of land.

Questions—State the distinction between public and private institutions. What is said of the Ohio Institution for the Education of Deaf Mutes? Of the State Asylum for the Education of Feeble-Minded and Imbecile Youth? Of the Ohio Institution for the Education of the Blind? Of the Northwestern Hospital for the Insane? Of the Western Ohio Hospital for the Insane?

CHAPTER XLIX.

BENEVOLENT INSTITUTIONS CONTINUED.

Central Ohio Hospital for the Insane.—The first building erected by the State for the insane was begun in 1835, and completed and occupied in 1839. The building was burned in 1868, and a new one is now being erected (1875) near Columbus on a site about three miles west from the old one. The total expenditures for this institution from 1835 to November 15, 1874, have been $2,171,729.45. The land now belonging to the institution, 300 acres, cost $100,000.

This, like other State institutions, is under the control of a board of trustees.

Northern Ohio Hospital for the Insane.—The State purchased for this institution fifty-six acres of land in 1852 at Newburgh for $2,300, and in 1870 fifty acres more for $16,800. The other expenditures to November 15, 1874 were, for buildings and betterments, $1,034,104.43, and for current expenses and repairs, $941,020.78; making the aggregate for all purposes $1,994,225.21.

South-Eastern Hospital for the Insane.—The land attached to this hospital, embracing 150 acres at Athens, was donated to the State in 1868.

The total expenditures to November 15, 1874, were $993,913.38. Of this, $899,188.62 were for buildings, permanent improvements and furniture, and $94,724.76 for current expenses and ordinary repairs.

Longview Lunatic Asylum.—This asylum belongs to Hamilton county. The expenses are borne jointly by the county and the State. Until April 28, 1873, the proportion paid by the State was equal to the amount annually raised by taxation from the county of Hamilton, for the support of lunatic asylums in the State. By an act of the General Assembly of that date, the apportionment of expenses afterward was to be on the basis of population.

Ohio Soldiers' and Sailors' Orphans' Home.—This home was established about December 1, 1869, and was sustained by private contributions until May 1, 1870, when the State took charge of it, with 115 children in attendance.

The land for this institution, 100 acres, near Xenia,

was donated in 1870. There have been expended by the State from 1870 up to November 15, 1874, for buildings and batterments, $245,463.15; for current expenses, $257,-507.58; for support of orphans outside of the Home, $4,490.85; and for wood land, $3,450 (the last two amounts paid in 1874); making the aggregate $510,911.58.

The Children's Home at 180 West Third street, Cincinnati, was established to provide temporary and permanent homes for neglected and homeless children. It does not keep the children who are committed to its care, in the institution for any time longer than may be necessary to secure suitable and permanent homes for them, with Christian people, in the country.

In is a chartered institution, and is carried on under the laws of the State of Ohio; by which it is authorized to receive the legal care and control of all children who are properly surrendered to it by their parents, guardians, or by the mayor of the city of Cincinnati. Over such, it acquires the authority and assumes the same responsibility as originally belonged to and devolved upon the parents.

It is supported entirely by voluntary subscriptions, and has no endowment fund or other dependance beyond the regular and occasional contributions of the friends of The Home, who sympathize with its objects and methods.

The German Methodist Orphan Asylum, at Berea, was founded in 1864, as a home for the orphans or other needy children of the German Methodist denomination, and others, so far as its means will permit.

The children are taught in the German and English languages and instructed in the branches of an elementary school. Special attention is given to their religious culture.

The Children's Home of Washington County is situated on the east bank of the Muskingum river, about one mile north of the corporation line of the city of Marietta.

The object of the institution is to furnish an asylum for indigent children of the county under 16 years of age, where they can be supported and provided with physical, mental and moral training, until suitable homes can be provided for them, or until they become capable of earning and providing for themselves, or their parents or guardians for them.

Children from other counties can also be admitted upon such terms as the trustees, and those having control of such children, may mutually agree upon.

The Protestant Orphans' Home, of Toledo, was organized in 1867. The organization consists of a society of persons, each of whom are required to contribute to its funds, annually, not less than five dollars. Those who pay the sum of fifty dollars at one time, are thereby constituted life members. The object of the society is the maintenance and education of orphans, half orphans and unprotected children.

It is under the management of a board of trustees, consisting of eighteen ladies, a majority of whom are required to be members of Protestant churches, and residents of the city of Toledo.

There are in the State numerous other charitable institutions, including poor houses and the like.

In all large cities there are institutions for the care of those who are unable to care for themselves. Some of these are supported by the municipalities in which they are located, while others are maintained by the voluntary offerings of those who live to do good and to brighten the pathway of the poor and unfortunate of our race.

Questions—Where is the Central Ohio Hospital for the Insane located? When was it erected? When destroyed? What has it cost? What is said of the Northern Ohio Hospital for the Insane? Of South-Eastern Hospital? Of Longview Asylum? Of the Ohio Soldiers' and Sailors' Orphans' Home? Of the Children's Home at Cincinnati? Of the German Methodist Orphan Asylumn at Berea? Of the Children's Home of Washington county? Of the Protestant Orphan's Home of Toledo? Of other charitable institutions?

CHAPTER L.

PENAL AND REFORMATORY INSTITUTIONS.

Penal and reformatory institutions have been found necessary for the punishment and reformation of those who commit crime. They are also necessary to restrain offenders, and thereby deprive them of the opportunity or power to violate the law.

The Ohio Penitentiary, established by the State, and

located at Columbus, is the institution to which persons convicted of the higher grade of offences—that is, those that are considered most atrocious and wicked—are sent for punishment.

The prison is under the management and government of three directors, appointed by the governor, by and with the consent of the senate.

The board of directors are required to appoint a warden, clerk, steward, physician, chaplain, and when business requires it, an assistant clerk.

The warden appoints a deputy warden, superintendents of the yard, kitchen, State shops and hospital, a captain of the night watch, and as many guards as may be necessary, subject to the right of the board at any time to order the number increased or diminished.

The general duties of the warden are.

1st. To carefully supervise the government, discipline and police of the prison.

2d. To give all necessary directions to the inferior officers and guards, and secure a careful and diligent discharge of their several duties.

3d. To examine daily into the state of the prison, and the health, condition and safety of the convicts.

4th. To report to the directors, at each quarterly meeting, the number of guards employed, their names and duties, and such other matters as may be required.

5th. And generally to have charge of all the departments of the prison and its officers, as its executive head.

Ohio Reform Farm School, located upon a farm of 1,170 acres, six miles south of Lancaster, Fairfield county, for the reception of boys under sixteen years of age, convicted of crime or misdemeanor, and sent by courts of record, ~~is a State institution and was opened in 1858~~.

Under certain restrictions, incorrigible boys may be sent to the reform school by parents or guardians.

The farm and improvements cost the State $180,000. The number of inmates range from 400 to 500.

At present the institution consists of eight family houses, each comfortably accommodating from fifty to sixty boys; a large and imposing central building for administrative and domestic purposes, ~~affording~~ rooms for the resident commissioner, guest chambers, offices, reading room, kitchens, dining halls for 500 boys, and dormitories for employes. There are also five shop buildings, four barns, an engine house, laundry building, water tower, gas works, bake house and a very fine and commodious chapel building that will comfortably seat 800 boys.

The boys attend school half of each day, and labor the other half.

While the commissioners impose no religious creed or dogma on the confiding and impressible minds of the boys, they are taught, by precept and example the moral and religious principles that underlie a good character.

In teaching them their duty to God, to themselves and their fellow-men, they train them to respect law and authority, and the great duty of self-government, so that in the trials of life they may maintain their integrity, stand firm in the day of temptation ~~and resist evil~~, live a pure, happy life, die honored and lamented, and be prepared for a joyous and exalted immortality.

The Girls' Industrial Home, located at White Sulphur Springs (Lewis Center), Delaware county, was erected by an act of the General Assembly, May 5th, 1869; to which girls, over seven and under sixteen years of age, may be committed for offences against the laws of the State, or who are leading idle, vagrant or vicious lives, or are found in circumstances of want and suffering, or of neglect, exposure, abandonment or beggary, and there kept, disciplined, instructed, employed and governed, till legally discharged.

The law makes provision for the establishment of jails in the several counties of the State. These jails are designed as places of punishment for persons convicted of minor offenses, and of detention for those who are held to await trial on charges of felony.

Prisons are established in cities and villages for the punishment of disorderly persons.

Questions—For what purposes are penal and reformatory institutions established? Where is the State penitentiary located? What class of offenders are confined in the penitentiary? What is said of the management and control of the penitentiary? Name its officers and state how they are appointed. What are the general duties of the Warden? Where is the reform farm school located? What persons are committed to the reform farm school? What did the farm and improvements cost the State? How many boys are there at this school? Describe the buildings. What is said of the labor and schooling of the inmates? What State institution has been provided for the care and reformation of girls? What is said of it? What class of girls are committed to it?

CRIMES AND MISDEMEANORS.

CHAPTER LI.

PUBLIC WRONGS—NECESSITY FOR PUNISHMENT—OFFENCES HOW CLASSIFIED.

The happiness of human beings depends largely upon the observance of certain rules and regulations in their relations with each other; and since some are unwilling to recognize and abide by these rules it has been found necessary to exercise power to enforce obedience to and acquiescence in them.

The remedy for wrongs or injuries that affect persons in their private capacity is by an action for the recovery of individual damages. But where the act is of such a nature as to endanger the public peace or morals, it is punished as a crime, and may also be redressed as a civil injury.

A crime is defined as "any act done by a person in violation of public duty that the law has directed to be done, or prohibited, and punishes its infraction."

In a limited sense, the word *crime* is confined to felony, that is, to those offences that are punishable by death or imprisonment in the penitentiary.

Misdemeanors include all offences inferior in grade to felonies.

The term *offence* is nearly synonymous with misdemeanor, but is usually applied to crimes not indictable, but punishable, summarily, or by the forfeiture of a penalty.

To enable the government to enforce the law against the commission of crimes, it is necessary to inflict punishment on offenders.

These punishments are designed to deter persons from violating the law, sometimes to furnish redress to the injured party, and always to hold out an example and induce reformation.

The statutes of this State classify crimes and misdemeanors as follows: Those which, on account of their atrocity, are by law made punishable by death or imprisonment in the penitentiary, are called crimes of the "first class;" those punishable generally by fines and imprisonment in county jails, or fine, or imprisonment, are called crimes of the "second class;" the "third class" consists of all minor offences.

Persons accused of crime have the right to counsel and witnesses in open court.

An *acquittal* on a trial of the facts is a bar to further prosecutions for the same offence.

Questions—What is said in regard to the happiness of human beings? Of the remedy for private wrongs? When it is of a public character? What is a crime? Misdemeanor? Offence? What is the design of punishment? How do the statutes of this State classify crimes and misdemeanors? What rights have persons accused of crime? What is said of an acquittal?

CHAPTER LII.

ABSTRACT OF THE CRIMINAL LAWS OF OHIO.*

In preparing an abstract of the criminal laws of Ohio we have sought perspicuity and at the same time brevity. In abbreviating, "p" is made to stand for "penitentiary"; "y" is made to stand for "year"; "mo" for "month"; "d" for "day"; "j" for "jail"; "j b w" for "jail on bread and water only"; "f" for "fine"; "ex" for "exceeding". These abbreviations will indicate the penalties for the offences enumerated in the abstract.

For laws prescribing punishment for those offences which are the offspring of lust, offences against chastity and decency, the student is referred to the statutes of the State. The punishment for such crimes is justly severe, being, in some cases, by imprisonment in the State penitentiary.

Though the places of imprisonment indicated in the statutes for the various offences, are either jail or the State penitentiary, it is provided by law that boys under

* It is deemed unnecessary to arrange questions for this chapter, as it is believed the proper questions will be readily suggested to the teacher, if it should be thought advisable to require pupils to commit the abstract.

sixteen years of age, of incorrigible or vicious conduct, or convicted of crime, may be sent to houses of refuge, or to the State reform farm school, near Lancaster, in Fairfield county.

Girls between the ages of seven and sixteen years, convicted of offences punishable by fine and imprisonment, other than imprisonment for life, or who are leading an idle, vagrant or vicious life, or who are found in any public place, in circumstances of want, may be sent to the reform school at White Sulphur Springs, in Delaware county, known as the Girls Industrial Home.

From the following it will be seen that the courts are vested with a large discretion as to the measure of punishment. This is necessary to enable them to do justice in view of the peculiar circumstances surrounding each case:

Abduction, fraudulently or forcibly carrying off or decoying out of the State, or unlawfully arresting and imprisoning any person, with the intention of having such person carried out of the State unlawfully, p 3 to 7 y, and costs of prosecution. [See Child Stealing.]

Abetting, aiding or procuring commission of felony; same punishment as principal offender.

Accessory in felony, same as abettor, &c.

Administration of justice, obstructing, f not ex $100, or j not ex 20 days, or both. [See Resisting—Riot--Officers.]

Adulterating. [See Milk—Liquors.]

Advertising lottery, f not ex $100.

Tearing down, defacing or destroying advertisements set up by legal authority, f not ex $10, and j not ex 24 hours.

Affray, by fighting or boxing at fisticuffs, f not ex $50 and j not ex 10 d, or both.

Persons who, in the presence of a magistrate, make an affray, threaten to kill or beat another, or to commit any offence against the person or property of another, or who shall indulge in angry words to the disturbance of the peace, may be ordered by such magistrate to give security in any sum not less than $50, nor more than $500, to appear before the court of common pleas on the first day of the next term, and in the meantime to keep the peace. Failing to give security, the offender may be sent to jail until discharged by due course of law. [See Riot.]

Africans, not to intermarry with white persons. [See White Persons.]

Animals—Maliciously injuring or killing animals of another, (unless to prevent trespass), to the value of $35, p 1 to 3 y. If value less than $35, f $5 to $200 or j not ex 3 mo, or both.—Killing such animals of the value of $35 by poison, p 1 to 7 y. If of less value than $35, f $20 to $200 and j not ex 3 mo. If animal thus poisoned does not die, f for administering the poison $100 or j b w not ex 30 d.—Selling diseased animals, knowingly, without disclosing fact of disease, or permitting them to run at large, f $20 to $200, and costs, or j not ex 30 d. Allowing same to come in contact with animals of others, without knowledge or permission of owner of such other animals, f $50 to $500 and costs, or j 10 to 50 d.—Suffering swine, being of the age of sixty days or more, to go at large, unless noses so cut or rings so inserted therein as to prevent their rooting, f $1 for each swine so found going at large.—Owner or keeper suffering vicious animals to go at large, f $5. Second or any subsequent conviction, $10.—Allowing horses, mules, cattle, sheep, goats, swine or geese, to run at large, without permission from county commissioners or township trustees, f $1 to $5.—Allowing dogs to run at large, not accompanied by persons having them in charge, f $5 and costs.—Torturing animals or aiding in same, f not ex $100.—Wrongful taking of horse, mare, gelding, foal or filly, ass or mule, with intent to injure, set at large, or wrongfully use such animal, f not ex $200, or j not ex 90 d, or both.—Permitting breechy animals to run at large, f 25 cts. each d. [See Game Law—Horse-racing—Horse-stealing.]

Apothecaries are required to make record of the name, age, sex and color of persons obtaining poisons from them; the quantity sold; the purpose for which it is required; the day and date on which it was obtained; name and place of residence of the person for whom it is intended; to mark the word "poison" on each package; to neither sell nor give away any poison to minors. Penalty for violation, f $20 to $200. (See Arsenic—Poison.)

Appraisers refusing to act as, when lawfully summoned, f 50 cents.

Apprentices, enticing away, harboring, or aiding to run away, f not ex $100.

Arrest, refusing to aid officer in making, f not ex $50.

Arsenic, not to be sold or given away in quantities less than one pound, without first mixing either soot or indigo therewith in the proportion of one ounce of soot or half a pound of indigo to a pound of arsenic, f $20 to $200.

Arson.—Burning buildings, bridges or watercraft, the property of another, of the value of $50, or containing property of the value of $50, or any public buildings, p 1 to 20 y. Attempting to commit arson by setting fire to such property with intent to burn or destroy it, p 1 to 7 y.—Burning of insured property of the value of $50, by the owner, with intent to prejudice insurer, p 1 to 20 y. Attempting to burn same, p 1 to 7 y.—Attempting to burn or ignite or communicate fire to property, the burning of which would be arson, though the same be not fired or burned, f not ex $300 or j b w not ex 4 mo.—Same attempt to ignite, set fire to or burn the Ohio penitentiary or its appurtenances, p 1 to 3 y. (See Burning—Fires.)

Assault, Menacing Threats, or Assault and Battery, f not ex $150, or j not ex 6 mo, and b w not ex 10 d, or both.—With intent to commit murder, rape or robbery, p 2 to 15 y.

Attempting to pass counterfeit coin or bank notes, knowing them to be counterfeit, p 1 to 5 y.

Auction, selling at, except utensils of husbandry and household furniture, real estate, produce, horses, sheep, hogs or neat cattle, without license, f $100 to $500. This law does not apply to judicial or other sales required by law.—Others than licensed auctioneers, selling at private sale at time and place where public auction is held, goods liable to auction duty, f equal to the amount for which the goods were sold.

Auctioneer failing to make out quarterly reports of business, to com. pleas court, f not ex $1,000, and forfeit license.—Farming out his office, f $100 to $1,000, and forfeit of license.

Ball or nine-pin alley, not to be kept or permitted on or in premises of keepers of public houses or retail liquor estalishments, f $10 to $100.

Ballot-boxes or ballots, obtaining or attempting to obtain unlawful possession of at election, p 1 to 3 y. Ballot-boxes, ballots or poll-boxes, unlawful distruction of, p 1 to 5 y. [See Election Law.]

Bank officers, clerks, etc., who embezzle, abstract or wilfully misapply funds or credits; or, without authority, issue notes, certificates of deposit, draw orders or bills of exchange, make any acceptance, assign any note, bond, draft, bill of exchange, mortgage, judgment or decree, or make any false entry on any book, report or statement of the company, with intent to injure or defraud, p 5 to 10 y. [See Bills of expired Banks—Embezzlement.]

Bars, gates or fences, maliciously opening or throwing down, f not ex $100 or j not ex 30 d, or both.

Bees—Stealing any contrivance containing honey or honey-bees, of less value than $35; or stealing therefrom, or maliciously disturbing, injuring or destroying same, f not ex $100, and j 10 to 30 d. Also liable in damages double value of actual injury.—Entering premises of another with intent to disturb bees or steal bees or honey, f not ex $500, or j not ex 60 d or both.

Betting on elections, f $5 to $500. Where the amount bet is between $5 and $500, the fine is equal to the amount hazarded by the bet.—Betting with minor or gaming with him for money or property f $50 to $200, or j 3 mo to 1 y.—Keeper of public place permitting minor under 18 years of age to be in or upon such premises, or to play upon billiard table, f $20, and for each succeding offence $50, with costs.

Bigamy.—If a married person, having a husband or a wife living, marry any other person, p 1 to 7 y. This law does not extend to any person whose husband or wife shall be continually and willfully absent for the space of five years together, and unheard from, next before the time of such marriage.

Bills or advertisements, posting, painting or printing of, on building, fence, wall or tree (except legal notices) without consent of owner, f $10 to $50.

Bills of expired banks, circulation of, prohibited under penalty, f not ex $500, or j not ex 30 d, or both.—Reissuing such paper, f not ex $1,000 or j not ex 30 d, or both.—Banking companies not to put in circulation their notes unless payable on demand and without interest. Officer or agent so doing may be punished by fine or imprisonment or both.

Bill of lading.—Executing, delivering, or causing to be executed or delivered, false or fictitious bill of lading, receipt, schedule, or invoice, with intent to injure or deceive; or indorsing, transferring or attempting to do so with fraudulent intent, p 1 to 4 y.

Birds and hares, unlawful killing of.—The law provides that it shall be unlawful for any person, at any time, to catch, kill or injure, or to pursue with such intent, on the premises of another, or on the public highways, streets, alleys, or public common any sparrow, robin, blue-bird, martin, thrush, mocking-bird, swallow, oriole, red-bird, cat-bird, chewink or ground robin, king-bird, bobolink, yellow-bird, pewee or phœbe, wren, cuckoo, indigo-bird, nut-hatch, creeper, yellow-hammer or flicker, warble or finch; or in any place to catch, kill or injure, or pursue with such intent, any quail or Virginia partridge, ruffled grouse or pheasant, or any wild turkey, between the first day of February and the 15th day of October, inclusive, or any pinnated grouse or prairie chicken, between the first day of February and the 15th of August. And it shall also be unlawful for any person at at time after the first day of February and before the first day of November, to catch, kill or injure, or pursue with such intent any dove, wild rabbit or hare, except on the premises of the person so killing, injuring, or pursuing; *provided*, that it shall be unlawful to catch or attempt to catch with a net or nets, snare or trap, any quail or Virginia partridge at any time after the passage of this act. [Act April 3, 1867, Swan and Sayler, 14.]

The law further provides that it shall be unlawful for any person at any time between the first day of February and the first day of October to catch, kill, injure or destroy, or pursue with such intent, any meadow-lark or kill-deer, or at any time between the first day of February and the fourth day of July, to catch, kill or injure, or pursue with such intent, any woodcock, or at any time between the 15th day of April and the first day of September to catch, kill or injure, or pursue with such intent, any wood-duck, teal or other wild duck, or to purchase and have in his possession, or expose for sale, any of the birds or game mentioned in this act, caught or killed during the season when the catching, killing, injuring, or destroying the same is hereby prohibited. It is also unlawful at any time, by the aid or use of any swivel, punt-gun, big-gun (so-called), or any gun other than the common shoulder gun, or by the aid or use of any punt-boat or sneak-boat used for carrying such gun, to hunt or kill any wild goose, wood-duck, teal, canvas back, blue-bill, or other wild duck. It is unlawful to disturb the eggs of any of the birds protected by this act. Penalty for violating any of the provisions of the bird law, f $2 to $20 and costs, or j not ex 20 d, or both.

Biting the person.—[See maiming.]

Board of Health.—Violating or interfering with the execution of lawful orders of, f not ex $100 or j not ex 90 d, or both. [See Health Officers.]

Brands and marks.—Falsely marking the weight on barrels, firkins, etc., or putting less therein than mark indicates, forfeit the cask, box, etc., and half its contents.—Maliciously defacing or altering brands or ear marks, f not ex $50, and liable in treble damages to party injured.

Breach of the peace, provoking, or attempting to provoke to, f $1 to $10. [See Affray—Riot.]

Breaking into mansion house, shop, store, ship, boat or other water-craft, in which any person shall reside or dwell, in the night time, and committing or attempting to commit any personal violence or abuse, or being so armed with any dangerous weapon, as to indicate a violent intention, f not ex $300 and j b w not ex 30 d.—Same offence in day time, f not ex $100 and j b w not ex 20 d, or both.—Breaking into buildings, boats, or cars in day time to steal, f not ex $300 and j b w not ex 60 d.

Entering building by night or day, and attempting to kill, disfigure, maim, rob, stab, or to commit rape or arson, or to aid or abet in the commission of any such offences, p 1 to 10 y. (See Burglary.)

Breach of trust, in making false statement by county treasurer and auditor as to property and money in treasury, penalty same as in embezzlement. (See Embezzlement.)

Bribery of officers or public agents, or attempts to bribe them with a view of influencing improperly their official action, or accepting, receiving or soliciting any reward for such purpose by such officer or agent, f not less than value of the thing promised or given, or so solicited or received, nor more than three times such value or amount, or j not ex 30 d, or both; and when the agent or officer is convicted, removal from office.—Attempting to corrupt or influence juror or witness by any undue means, f not ex $500 and j not ex 30 d.—Juror or witness corruptly receiving reward, f not ex $500 and j b w not ex 30 d.—To give or promise any valuable thing to influence judgment of judge, justice or arbitrator, f $50 to $1,000.—Bribing officer or others to procure escape of criminal, f $25 to $200.

Bridge, malicious distruction of, f not ex $500 or j b w not ex 30 d or both.

Bridges and Landmarks, destruction of, f not ex $500 or j b w not ex 30 d, or both.

Brothel—Renting a house or building to be used as a brothel or permitting it so to be used, f not ex $100, or j 30 d to 6 mo or both.

Bullets, playing same across any street in any town or village f 50 cts to $5.

Burglary.—If any person shall, in the night, willfully, maliciously, and forcibly, break and enter into any dwelling-house, kitchen, smoke-house, shop, office, store-house, ware-house, malt-house, still-house, mill, pottery, factory, water craft, school-house, church or meeting-house, barn or stable, railroad car factory, station house or railroad car, with intent to kill, rob, commit a rape, or with intent to steal property of any value, or to commit any act made criminal by the act of March 7th, 1835, or acts amendatory thereto, p 1 to 10 y. [See Breaking.]

Burning.—Setting fire to or causing to be burned, any barrack or stack of hay, wheat, rye, oats, barley, flax, hemp, fodder, grain, corn-crib, or place where corn may be deposited, or any fence, boards, plank, scantling rails, tan-bark or timber of another, of the value of thirty-five dollars, or upwards, p 1 to 3 y. If injury or damage less than thirty-five dollars, f $5 to $100 or j not ex 30 d or both. [See Arson—Fires.]

Camp Meeting.—Articles of traffic not to be sold within four miles of, without permit from managers of the society or assemblage, except at regular place of business, f $10 to $100. [See Liquors.]

Canada Thistles.—Owners of land permitting Canada thistles to go to seed thereon, or on adjoining highway, f $10.—Knowingly vending grass or other seed containing Canada thistle seed, f $20.

Cannon, firing of, or exploding or causing to be exploded at any one time more than four ounces of gunpowder, except in case of invasion or to suppress insurrections, or mobs, or for the purpose of raising drowned human bodies, or for the purpose of blasting or removing rock, upon any public street or nearer than ten rods to the same, f $5 to $50.

Carnal knowledge of insane woman by person seventeen years old and upward, other than his wife, knowing her to be insane, p 3 to 10 y. [See Adultery—Fornication—Rape—Incest—Illicit Carnal Intercourse.]

Cheese. [See Milk.]

Child Stealing, where child is under ten years of age, or aiding in the commission of the offence, or knowingly harboring or concealing such child, with intent to detain it from its parents or guardian, p 1 to 7 y.

Cock-fighting, exhibiting or assisting, f not ex $20.

Coin, spurious, selling or disposing of, or having the same in possession with intent to sell or dispose of same, p 1 to 10 y.

Concealing stolen goods, money, etc., knowingly, of less value than $35, f not ex $200, or j b w not ex 30 d, or both.

Constable, neglecting to serve warrant in cases of crimes of the first-class, when in his power to serve the same, f not ex $500, or j not ex 10 d, or both, and forfeiture of his office. For same neglect in cases of minor offences, f not ex $100, or j not ex 10 d, or both, and forfeiture of his office.

Counterfeit, spurious bank notes or coin, having in possession, knowingly, p 1 to 10 y.—Counterfeiting coin, altering or knowingly putting off such coin, or making or keeping instruments to counterfeit coin, disposing of or having in posesion knowingly, forged bank notes, filled up or in blank; making, publishing or altering notes of a fictitious bank, p 3 to 15 y.—Counterfeiting notes, bonds, postage currency, or other securities issued by the United States, f not ex $5,000, and p not ex 15 y.—Having in custody or using counterfeit stamps, plates, notes, etc., or engraving or conniving at engraving, vending or selling the same, or printing, or photographing the same, except by proper authority, f not ex $5,000, and p not ex 15 y. [See Engraving—Attempting.]

County Commissioners, or persons employed by them to superintend, in whole or in part, work on court house, infirmary, jail or bridge, or the making plans, specifications, and estimates, guilty of fraud in relation to such work, f $100 to $1000, and j 3 to 6 mo, and liable to county for double damages.

Defacing, injuring or destroying newspapers, magazines, etc. belonging to the State or any association, or cutting therefrom any article or advertisement, f $10 to $100, or j not ex 30 d, or both.

Diseased Animals. [See Animals.]

Disturbance. Wilfully disturbing any school or society organized by law or convened for intellectual improvement, etc., or social amusement, f $5 to $20, and costs, and be imprisoned until paid, not ex 5 d.—Of other than religious meetings, f 50 cts to $5. [See Religious Meetings.]

Dogs. [See Animals.]

Duelling, challenging, encouraging, accepting or bearing challenge, or acting as second in duel, p 1 to 10 y, and rendered incapable of holding any office of profit or trust; and if death ensue, all parties concerned deemed guilty of murder.

Election laws, offences against.—Voting out of one's own proper ward, township or village, f $200 to $500 and j 3 to 6 mo.—Voting out of one's own proper county, p 1 to 3 y.—Voting more than once at same election, p 1 to 5 y.—Non-resident of State voting in this State 1 to 5 y.—Not having resided a year in the State, not being twenty-one years of age, not being a citizen of the U. S., or being convict and not restored to rights of an elector, and voting, j 1 to 6 mo.—Aiding, advising or procuring another to vote unlawfully, f $100 to $500, and j 1 to 6 mo.—Aiding, advising or procuring another to go into another county than his own to vote, p 1 to 5 y.—Bribing or threatening a voter, to influence his vote, or to deter him from giving his vote or ballot, f $100 to $500 and j 1 to 6 mo.—[See Swan and Critchfield's Statutes, 540.]—Deceiving elector who cannot read, by furnishing him with ticket, informing him that it contains names different from those written or printed thereon, or fraudulently or deceitfully changing a ballot of an elector so as to prevent him from voting as he intended, p 1 to 3 y.—Fraudulently putting ticket or ballot into ballot-box by elector or election judge, p 1 to 3 y.—False swearing as to qualification to vote, same as for other perjury.—Judges and clerks of election for wilful violation of official duty, f $100 to $1,000, and j 3 to 6 mo.—Persons convicted and sentenced to penitentiary under this act, or for bribery, are thereby rendered incompetent to be elector, or to hold office, unless pardoned by the governor.—Ballots not to be fraudulently marked by any person, and to be on plain white paper, without mark or device. Printing of ticket with names therein other than those on regular ticket, prohibited.—Penalty for violating provision as to ballots, f $10 to $50, and j not ex 10 d, and liable to a civil action by any elector for a penalty of $100.—No spiritous, vinous, or malt liquors to be disposed of in any manner on election days, f $5 to $100 and j not ex 10 d.

Electors, privileges of forfeited.—(See Sentence—Fees.)

Embezzlement of money, goods, rights in action, or other valuable security or effects, or making way with or secreting same with intent to embezzle, by clerk or servant, (except apprentices, and persons within the age of eighteen years), or by officer or agent, penalty same as for larceny of property of equal value.—Embezzlement by carriers of goods, moneys or effects, same as larceny.—Inn-keeper converting money, notes, jewelry, articles of gold or silver, precious stones, or bullion, deposited by guests, same as larceny.—Embezzlement of public money, what acts deemed. (See Swan and Critchfield, 1610.)—Fraudulent appropriation of merchandise by factor or agent, p 1 to 3 y.—Frauds by consignors of goods, upon their consignees, by disposing of merchandise contrary to agreement, after receiving advances thereon from consignee, p 1 to 3 y: *Provided*, no person shall be subject to penalty, who, before disposing of such merchandise shall pay or offer to pay full amount of such advancement. (See Receipts.)

[For other frauds, concerning appropriation of merchandise, see statutes, Swan and Critchfield, 432.—See Freight—Elections—Partner—Bank Officer—Insolvent—Municipal Officer.]

Engraving, or keeping plate for counterfeiting or altering bank notes or bills, or knowingly having in possession and secretly keeping the same for the purpose of counterfeiting, p 3 to 15 y.

Escape—Person having custody of offender voluntarily permitting him to escape, f not ex $500, or j not ex 10 d, or both.—(See Guards.)

Extortion.—(See Ministerial Officers.)

Falsely personating another, before officer authorized to take acknowledgement of deeds, powers or warrants of attorney, or to grant marriage licenses with intent to defraud, p 1 to 6 y.

Fees.—Judicial or ministerial officer knowingly demanding or receiving unlawful fees, f. not ex $200 or j b. w. not ex 10 d., or both, and for seven years thereafter be incapable of holding office.

Fences, throwing down. [See Bars.]

Ferrymen neglecting to discharge their duties faithfully, f not ex $5.—For receiving excessive sum for ferriages, f $10.—Keeping ferry without license, f not ex $30.

Fighting at fisticuffs by agreement, f not ex $50 or j not ex 10 d. or b. [See Affray.]

Firearms, discharging on or within one hundred yards of cemetery, unless upon land of owner, f not ex $20 and costs, or j 10 d, or both. [See Cannon—Game Laws.]

Fires, maliciously setting to woods, prairies, or other grounds, other than his own, or intentionally permitting fires to pass from his own to the injury of any other person or persons, f not ex $50, and be imprisoned until fine paid; also liable for damages. [See Arson—Burning.]

Fish. [See Nuisance.]

Forgery.—Falsely making, uttering, forging, counterfeiting, printing, photographing, or falsely uttering or publishing any of the records or instruments enumerated in the statute [See Supplement to Revised Statutes of Ohio, by Swan and Sayler, p. 264] and which embrace nearly every public or private document which would represent property, or furnish evidence of any interest therein, or of any legal obligation, or release therefrom, p 3 to 20 y.

Forging stamps, brands, labels or trade marks, knowingly, or having same or plate, etc., in possession, j 3 to 12 mo and f not ex $500.—Vending or keeping for sale articles having forged stamps, brands, labels or trade marks, etc., f not ex $100. Complainant entitled to half the fine recovered.

Justices of the peace are authorized to seize and destroy false dies, brands, and plates, on being satisfied that they are to be used for the purposes of deception and fraud.

The fraudulent use of brands and stamps upon merchandise,

or the erasing, transferring or concealing the same for the purpose of fraud, f $20 to $60, or j 30 to 60 d. Second offence, $50 to $200, or j 60 to 90 d, or both. Third offence, $200 to $500, or j 90 d to 6 mo, and in every instance to pay all expenses, prosecutions, costs and damages.

Fraudulent transfers of property to cheat creditors, f not ex $500, or j b w not ex 10 d, or both.

Freight.—Railroad company, by agent, knowingly diverting or permitting to be diverted, freight, on different line than that ordered, forfeits three times the amount received for transporting such freight, and guilty agent f not ex $100 or j not ex 30 d, or both.

Fruit or other trees of another, in nursery, garden, yard or orchard, malicious injury to, f $5 to $500, and liable in double damages to injured party.—Cutting, boxing, or injuring other trees of another, f $5 to $100 and liable in double damages to the party injured.—Malicious injury to ornamental trees in street or public grounds, f $5 to $100 and liable to double damages to the party injured. [See Trees.]

Gambler.—Being a common gambler, that is one who keeps or exhibits any gaming table, device or apparatus to win or gain money or other property, or who aids, assists or permits others to do the same, or who engages in gambling for a livelihood, j 1 to 6 mo and f not ex $500.

Game.—Hunting or killing deer between Oct. 1st and Jan. following, or to have in possession or expose to sale said game within such time, f $30 to $60, or j 10 to 30 d, or both.—Killing, trapping or hunting muskrat, mink or otter on lands of another, between April 5th and Feb. 15th following (except where there is danger of their doing injury to property), without owner's consent, or injuring muskrat heaps, or houses, without consent of owner of premises, f $2 to $25 and costs, and traps forfeited to owner of premises on which they may have been set. [For laws concerning unlawful fishing see Swan and Sayler's Supplement to Statutes 16; or Warren's Criminal Law, 3d ed., 377.—See Birds.]

Gaming and Betting.—Playing at any but games of athletic exercise, at any public place, or betting on the hands or sides, of such as do play, f not ex $100.—Money won by gaming or betting may be recovered by the loser.—Playing games or betting for money, f not ex $100, or j 10 d to 6 mo.—Keeping or exhibiting gaming device or billiard table for gain, f $50 to $200, and to give security for good behavior for one year in the sum of $500.—Suffering game to be played for gain on premises, f $50 to $200.—Keeper of public house suffering gaming at such house, other than athletic exercise, f $50 to $200, and forfeit of license.—Keeping gambling room or place for gambling, or allowing one's own premises or place to be used for such purpose, f $30 to $500, or j 10 to 30 d, or both.

Gilding current silver coin or other metal, so as to give it the appearance of gold coin; passing any such false or gilded money, knowing it as not genuine, p 1 to 5 y.

Grave or tomb of deceased person, openeng of, or removal of body from, without consent of near relatives of deceased, or proper legal authorities; or in any way aiding or procuring the same to be done, or to aid in any surgical or anatomical experiments with such body, knowing the same to have been so taken or removed, f not ex $1,000, or imprisonment not ex 6 mo.

Guards or other officers of penitentiary assisting, or attempting to assist or persuade prisoners to escape, p not longer than escaped prisoner sentenced for.—Conveying or abetting, or procuring to be conveyed to any convict therein, or attempting so to do, any weapon, ammunition or other thing without authority, p 2 to 10 y. [See Escape.]

Gun Powder. [See Cannon.]

Harboring or concealing thief or robber, knowing him or her to be such, p 1 to 7 y.

Health, offenses against.—Producing stagnant water, injurious to public health, f n ex $500, and nuisance to be abated.—Putting carcass of dead animal into water, of which use is made for domestic purposes, f 2 to $40.—Putting or leaving the carcass of any dead animal, offals from slaughter house or butcher's establishment, packing house or fish house, or any spoiled meats or spoiled fish, putrid animal substance, or contents of any privy vault, upon or into any river, bay, creek, pond, canal, road, street, alley, lot, field, meadow, public ground, market space, or common; or if owner or occupant of premises knowingly permit the same to remain thereon, to the annoyance of any citizen, or shall neglect or refuse to remove or abate the nuisance within twenty-four hours after knowledge or notice of such nuisance, f $1 to $50 and costs; and if not abated, each twenty-four hours thereafter shall be deemed a new offence.—Keepers of distilleries permitting their hog styes to become unclean between the 1st of April and the 1st of October, to the annoyance of any citizen, f $5 to $50 and costs. If not then abated, each five days, after institution of suit, deemed separate offence.—Erecting, keeping up or continuing any nuisance, to the injury of any part of the citizens, f not ex $500, and nuisance to be abated.—Person in charge of cemetery suffering dead body to remain in any vault, or other receptacle, until the same shall become offensive, f not ex $20 and $5 for every day thereafter that nuisance shall be continued.—Catching fish for salting and packing for market, or to salt and pack the same for market, between June 1st and September 1st, f $50 to $200.

Hogs. [See Animals.]

Horse racing in public road, in common use, f $1 to $5 and costs. In town or village, 50 cents to $5.

Horse stealing.--Stealing any horse, mare, gelding, foal or filly, ass or mule, or knowingly receiving or buying same to defraud owner; or concealing same, or the thief, knowingly, p 3 to 15 y.

House breaking. [See Burglary--Breaking.]

Indecent exposure of person, or use of obscene language in presence or hearing of female, f not ex $5, or j b w not ex 10 d, or both.

Injuries to buildings, or contents.—Malicious injury to building, its fixtures, books or appurtenances, or committing nuisance therein, or trespass upon the enclosure, or sidewalk, or fixtures thereto, f not ex $100, and imprisoned until fine paid or discharged by law. [See Malicious Injury.]

Insolvent.—Fraud by petitioner for relief, under insolvent laws, by concealing or disposing of property to defraud creditors, f not ex $500, or j b w not ex 10 d, or both.

Insurance company.—Fraudulently obtaining, or attempting to obtain, from life or accident insurance company, any money on policy, f not ex $500, or j not ex 6 m, or both. [For particulars, see Swan and Sayler's Supplement, p. 273.]

Intoxicated.—Persons found intoxicated, f $5.—Administering medicine when intoxicated, so as to endanger life, f not ex $100. [See Liquors.]

Jail keeper, permitting jail to become unclean, so as to endanger health of prisoners, f not ex $100.

Judge of Court of Common Pleas, acting as attorney in Justice's Court, f $5 to $200, j b w 10 to 30 d.

Judicial or ministerial officers, stirring up or encouraging suits, quarrels, etc., f not ex $500, and answerable to party injured in treble damages.

Kidnapping. [See Abduction.]

Land, selling or conveying without title, with intent to defraud, p 1 to 7 y.

Land-marks, maliciously cutting, felling, defacing, altering, or removing, f not ex $500, or j b w not ex 30 d or both.

Larceny—Stealing of money or goods of less value than $35, or stealing or maliciously destroying any money, promissory note, bill of exchange, or draft, receipt, warrant, check, or bond, given for the payment of money, or receipt acknowledging the receipt of money, or other property, of less value than $35, f not ex $200 or j not ex 30d, or to perform hard labor under regulation of county commissioners, or all of such punishments, and make restitution in two-fold the amount of property stolen or destroyed. Where property exceeds $35 in value, p 1 to 7 y.

Letters, sending or delivering of, to extort money or other valuable things, or threatening injury, f $50 to $500, or j b w not ex 10 d, or both.

Libel.—Publishing or printing malicious libel of or concerning another, or causing or procuring same, f not ex $500 or j not ex 6 m.

Liquor, intoxicating, selling of to Indians, f $25 to $100, and forfeit of articles received for such liquor.—Selling to be drank in or about premises where sold; selling to minors, unless upon written order of parents, guardian, or physician; selling to persons intoxicated or in the habit of becoming intoxicated, f $5 to $50, or j 10 to 30 d, or both.—Keeping a room or building where liquor is sold in violation of law, such places declared nuisances, to be shut up and abated, until keeper furnish security in sum of $1,000, not to sell liquors contrary to law, and to pay all fines, costs and damages assessed against him therefor. Giving away or other shift to evade the law deemed to be unlawful selling.—Buying or furnishing liquor for a minor or for a person intoxicated or in the habit of getting so, unless given by physician in regular line of practice, f $10 to $100 or j 10 to 30 d or both.—Selling or offering liquors within four miles of camp meeting, f $10 to $100.—Selling liquors at or within two miles of agricultural fairs, and not desisting when notified, f $5 to $50, to be paid for the benefit of such agricultural society.—Adulterating liquors, selling same, or selling liquors not inspected, contrary to law, f $100 to $500 and j 1 to 30 d.—Putting adulterated liquor into casks marked pure by inspector, or offering same for sale for purpose of deceiving, p not ex 1 y. Law not to apply to druggists, physicians and persons engaged in the mechanical arts, for adulterating liquors for medical and mechanical purposes.—Using strychnine or other poison in the manufacture or preparation, by rectifying or otherwise, any intoxicating or alcoholic liquors, or selling such poisoned liquors, p 1 to 5 y.—Manufacturers of liquors to label casks with these words: "Containing no poisonous drug or other added poison." If manufacturers found in possession of vessels containing liquors poisoned or not legally branded, f not ex $100 for each vessel containing same, and j 1 to 6 mo, and liquors to be destroyed.—Unlawful to convey liquors into jail unless prescribed by physician, f $10 to $100, or j 10 to 30 d.

Persons injured in person, property, or means of support by reason of intoxication of any person, have a right of action against the seller who caused the intoxication, for their damages. [See Intoxication—Rioting—Election Laws.

Lottery.—Making, drawing or being concerned in lottery or scheme of chance, as agent or owner, fine not ex $500, or be imprisoned not ex 6 mo, or both.—Advertising same, f not ex $10.

Magazines. [See Defacing.]

Maiming or disfiguring another, with malicious intent, p 1 to 20 y.

Malicious injury to the amount of $100 to personal property or building of another, p 1 to 3 y, and liable to party injured in double the amount of injury sustained.—To any amount less than $100, j not ex 30 d, and f double the amount of the injury.—To the amount of $35 or upwards, to any salt well, salt furnace or engine connected therewith, p 1 to 3 y, and liable io the party injured in double the amount of injury sustained. [See Mileston—Monument—Trees--Turnpikes—Animals.]

Manslaughter, unlawfully killing another, without malice, while the slayer is in the commission of some unlawful act, p 1 to 10 y.

Marriage.—Marriage certificates to be returned to the probate judge, within three months after marriage, by justice or minister. Neglect to do so, f $50.—Probate judge neglecting to record same, f $50.—Justice or minister marrying persons contrary to law, f not ex $1,000.—Persons not authorized, attempting to solemnize marriage, f $500.—Enticing husband or wife to join any sect whose principles or practice inculcate abandonment of wives and children, or renunciation of matrimonial contract, f not ex $500. Penalty not to extend to person for delivering any public sermon, exhortation or address.—Marriage of blacks and whites. [See White Persons.]

Medicine, administrating of, avowing it to be a secret, and thereby endangering life, f not ex $100. [See Intoxicated.]

Meetings. [See Disturbance.]

Milestone or guide-board, malicious injury to, or destruction of, f not ex $50, or j not ex 10 d, or both.

Military Expeditions against other States, beginning, setting on foot of, or providing means for, p 1 to 10 y. [See Treason.]

Milk and Cheese.—It is provided by law that whoever shall knowingly sell, to any person or persons, or, deliver or bring to be manufactured to any cheese or butter manufactory in this State, any milk diluted with water, or in any way adulterated, or milk from which any cream has been taken, or milk commonly known as "skimmed milk," or shall keep back any part of milk known as "strippings," with intent to defraud, or shall knowingly sell milk, the product of diseased animal, or animals, or shall knowingly use any poisonous or deleterous material in the manufacture of cheese or butter, f $25 to $100, and be liable in double damages to the party injured.

Miller, or mill owner, duty of, in putting up or packing flour. Duty to brand on head of each barrel the quality of flour therein, and the initial letter of his christian name, and his sir name in full; or if mills owned by more than one, then names of owners or company. For neglecting so to do, f $5.—Packing bran, shorts, middlings or unmerchantable flour with intent to defraud, f $100 to $500.

Ministerial Officers corruptly or maliciously injuring others, under color of office, or attempting so to do, f not ex $200, and treble damages for injury inflicted.

Monument or Tombstone, malicious injury to, f not ex $200 and j b w not ex 30 d.—By acts of April 17, 1857, wilful injury to cemetery property of any kind, f $5 to $500, or j 1 to 30 d.

Municipal Officer misapplying funds of the corporation, knowingly, f $100 to $1,000, or j 20 d to 6 mo, or both.

Murder, in the first degree, the killing of another purposely, and of deliberate and premeditated malice, or in the perpetration or attempt to perpetrate any rape, arson, robbery or burglary, or by administering poison or causing the same to be done. Penalty death.

Murder, second degree, killing of another purposely and maliciously, but without deliberation and premeditation, p during life.

Muskingum River, or its navigable branches, obstruction of, so as to prevent or impede the full passage of water-craft, f not ex $50, or j not ex 10 d, or both.

Muskrats.—[See Game.]

Newspapers.—[See Defacing.]

Notices, defacing.—[See Advertisement.]

Obscene Language.—[See Indecent Exposure of Person.]

Obtaining money or goods by false pretenses, f not ex $500 or j b w not ex 10 or both.

Office, usurpation of, or oppression in, f not ex $250 or j b w not ex 10 d or both.

Officers failing to discharge duty as required by act of Feb. 28th, 1831 (S. and C. 654.) f not ex $50.—[See Judicial—Refusing —Resisting—Surveyor.]

Oppression in Office.—[See Ministerial—Office.]

Partner.—Fraud by one member of firm upon another in regard to partnership matters, f not ex $500, or j not ex 6 mo or both.

Peace—Persons threatening to commit offenses against the person or property of another may, on complaint, be arrested and required to enter into a recognizance to appear before the court of common pleas at its next term, and in the mean time to keep the peace.—[See Affray.]

Perjury.—False oath or affirmation in proceedings or matters required by law, p 3 to 10 y.—Persuading or procuring another to commit perjury, p 3 to 10 y.—[See Election Laws.]

Subornation of Perjury.—[See Perjury.]

Poison, administerating to another, with intent to injure, or mixing same with water, food, drink, or medicine, with same intent, p 2 to 15 y.—[See Apothecary—Intoxicated—Arsenic—Muder —Animals—Liquor.]

Ponds.—Producing artificial ponds, or stagnant waters, to the injury of the public health, f not ex $500, and the nuisance to be abated or removed.

Pounds, unlawful interference with, f not ex $50 and costs or j not ex 10 d, or both.

Prisoners. — Furnishing disguise or instruments, etc., to prisoners to enable them to escape, whether successful or not, f $50 to $500, or j not ex 3 mo, or both.—[See Escape—Guards—Sheriff or Jailor.]

Profane Swearing, f 25 cts to $1.

Provisions—Unwholesome, selling of, knowingly, f not ex $50.

Prize Fighting—P 1 to 10 y, and costs of prosecution—Aiders and abettors, f $50 to $500, and j 10 d to 3 mo, and costs.

Puppet show, wire dancing, tumbling or sleight of hand for money, f $10.

Railroad Companies—Refusing to obey order of railroad commissioner as to speed of trains on defective track, etc., f not ex $500, or j not ex 1 y, or both—Railroad engineer failing to stop train when, and as required by law, f $100, and if death result from such neglect, he is deemed guilty of manslaughter.—If bodily injury result not affecting life, j 1 to 20 mo or f not ex $500, or both.—Permitting animals to enter enclosure of railroad, or to drive them within such enclosure upon the track, at any other place than regular crossings, or to place within such enclosure or upon such railroad track, any feed, salt, or other inducement for animals to enter such enclosure, f not ex $10 for first offense, and $30 for each additional offense.—Each ten hours animal permitted to remain on track deemed a separate offense.—Drawing or driving carriage, wagon, cart, coach, gig, or other two or four-wheeled vehicle, between the rails or track, or on or along the graded roadway of such railroad, unless compelled by necessity so to do, f $5 to $25, to be collected and paid over for use of railroad company.—Wilful and malicious injury to railroads, their fixtures, equipments or buildings, to the value of $35, or upwards, p 1 to 3 y.—If value less than $35, f $5 to $100, or j b w not ex 30 d, or both.—Aiders and abettors punished same as principals—By statute of 1863, punishment for injuring railroads or obstructing track, p 1 to 20 y; and if death of any person or persons be occasioned by such offence, the offender deemed guilty of murder.

Receipts,—Executing and delivering false receipts that goods are received at any place, with intent to defraud, p 1 to 3 y.

Receiving or buying goods of the value of $35, or upwards, knowingly, with intent to defraud the owner, p 1 to 7 y.—If of less value than $35, f not ex $200, and j b w not ex 30 d.—Receiving or buying bank bills, bonds, receipts or other property of the value of $35 and upwards, knowing them to be stolen, p 1 to 7 y. If of less value than $35, f not ex $200 and j b w not ex 30 d. [See Larceny.]

Refusing to aid officer in arresting and securing criminal, f not ex $50.

Religious Meetings, disturbing of,—Offender may be ejected from the place of worship, and fined not ex $20.—[See Disturbance.]

Rescue, by force, of criminal, or person charged with crime, from prison or keeper, f not ex $500, and j b w not ex 30 d.—Assisting prisoner to escape, though no escape be made, f $50 to $500, or j not ex 30 d, or both.—[See Escape.]

Resisting or abusing judicial or ministerial officers, in the execution of their office, f not ex $200, or j b w not ex 20 d, or both. —[See Riot—Officer.]

Riot.—Three or more persons assembled together with intent to do unlawful act against the person or property of another, or against the peace; or, being lawfully assembled, agree with each other to do unlawful act, f not ex $200, and j b w not ex 10 d.

It is the duty of judges and other peace officers to warn rioters to disperse, and they may call to their aid the power of the county. Persons refusing to assist, f not ex $25.—Obstructing authorities, or continuing together after proclamation made to disperse, or attempted to be made, and prevented by rioters, or in case of no proclamation, three or more persons so assembled commit unlawful act, f not ex $500, and j b w not ex 30 d, and shall find security for good behavior, and to keep the peace not exceeding one year.—See Affray—Resistng.

Rioting, revelling or drunkenness permitted in or on premises of tavern keeper, subjects keeper to f not ex $100.

Robbery.—Taking from person of another personal property of any value, forcibly and by violence, or by putting in fear, with intent to rob or steal, p 3 to 15 y.

Sabbath, observance of.—Sporting, rioting, quarrelling, hunting, fishing or shooting on the Sabbath, f not ex $20, or j not ex 20 d, or both.—Laboring on Sabbath, (work of necessity and charity only excepted) $1 to $5.—Law prohibiting labor not to extend to those who conscientiously observe Saturday as the Sabbath, nor to prevent families moving, watermen from landing passengers, keepers of toll-bridges or gates, from attending same, or ferrymen from conveying travelers over the waters.

Salt-Wells.—[See Malicious Injury.]

Second-hand Goods Dealers in cities of first and second class, required to keep up sign giving name and occupation, and to enter in a book, date, description of goods purchased, and name, age and residence of seller.—Not to buy of minors or apprentices, second-hand goods, nor from any one between 9 at night and 7 in the morning, f not ex $500.

Sentence of Imprisonment.—Persons sentenced to p under act of March 7th, 1835, [See statutes, Swan and Critchfield, 401] which embraces most penitentiary offences, are thereby disfranchised and rendered incompetent to be an elector unless pardoned by the governor, or unless sentence be reversed or annulled. Persons also disfranchised who have been imprisoned in the penitentiary of any other State or Territory of this Union under a sentence for the commission of any crime which by the laws of this State is punishable by imprisonment in the penitentiary.

Sheep, diseased, owner of, allowing them to run at large, knowing the same to be diseased, or selling same without disclosing the fact, f $20 to $100.

Sheriff or Jailor dealing with prisoner less severely than sentence warrants, except in cases of sickness, f not ex $100.

Shooting, stabbing, cutting or shooting at another maliciously, with intent to kill, wound or maim such person, p 1 to 20 y.—[See Target—Cannon.]

Sleight-of-Hand.—[See Puppet Show.]

Stabbing.—[See Shooting.]

Stealing.—[See Larceny.]

Stirring up Suits, etc.—[See Judicial, etc.]

Surveyor, improperly hindering or interfering with while engaged in official duties, f not ex $100.

Swine.—[See Animals.]

Target, shooting at, within any recorded town plat, f 50 cts to $5. [See Shooting.]

Tavern-keepers, harboring intoxicated Indians, f $5 to $25. [See Ball Alleys—Liquor.]

Thief. [See Harboring.]

Toll, for grinding grain, taking unlawful, f not ex $20.

Toll-Gate, injury to. [See Turnpike.]

Treason.—Persons residing in this State are deemed guilty of offense who *levy* war against this State, or the United States, or adhere to their enemies, giving them aid and comfort. Penalty death.

Accessories to treason, that is, those who help to commit the crime, or who knowingly conceal the same, p 10 to 20 y. [See Military Expeditions.]

Trees standing or growing in any orchard, nursery, grove or forest, of the value of $35, or upwards, malicious injury to, p 1 to 10 y, and offender liable in double damages sustained by owner.—Severing or carrying away timber, trees, growing or standing poles, or any cultivated root, plant, or other vegetable, in such manner as that the taking would amount to larceny if severed, or advising or directing, with intent to defraud the owner or injure him in his property, f not ex $200 or j b w not ex 30 d and costs; and liable to owner in double damages.—Unlawfully, willfully and maliciously severing or injuring trees, vines, shrubs, etc., on premises of another, or on public streets or grounds, f not ex $500, or j not ex 60 d, or both.—The statute of April 13, 1865, makes the penalty for destroying or injuring trees, shrubs or vines on street or elsewhere, f not ex $150 or j 5 to 30 d, or both, and makes the offender liable in treble damages.—Trees growing on lands of the State, or incorporated company, or private person, not to be cut or injured without lawful authority, under penalty of $1 to $100, or j not ex 20 d, or both.

Trespassing upon the lands of another while mining for coal or other minerals, willfully and without authority, f $5 to $100, or j not ex 10 d or both. If trespass continued, each twenty-four hours deemed an additional offence. Aiders and abettors same punishment. [See Trees—Railroads.]

Turnpike Bridges.—Fire not to be carried across wooden bridge or turnpike unless in lantern or close vessel, f $5—Riding or driving over such bridge faster than a walk, f $2.—United States mail not subject to such penalty.

Turnpike Road or appurtenances, malicious injuries to, f $10 to $50, and liable in double damages.—Depositing materials on roads inside of ditches, or so near as to cause banks to break into same, or cause accumulation of rubbish, f $5.

Waterwheels near public highways, to be covered so as to prevent same from frightening horses.—For failure so to do, f not ex $50 and costs.

Weapons, concealed, carrying of, unless under peculiar circumstances, justifying it; first offense, f not ex $200, or j not ex 30 d; second offense, f not ex $500 or j not more than three months, or both.

Weights, marking of.—Failure to weigh and mark tear and nett on boxes, etc., containing articles sold by weight, and not subject to inspection by law, f $20 to $60, or j 30 to 60 d; second offense, $50 to $200, or j 30 to 90 d, or both; third offense, $200 to $500, j 90 d to 6 mo, and in every instance all expenses, prosecutions, costs and damages.

Weights and Measures.—Fraud in weighing or measuring, f not ex $50, or j not ex 30 d, or both, and liable in double damages.

White Persons, (of pure white blood) not to inter-marry or have carnal intercourse with persons having visible admixture of African blood. Penalty for both or either, f not ex $100, or j not ex 3 mo or both. Penalty for solemnizing such marriage, or issuing license therefor, knowingly, f not ex $100, or j not ex 3 mo, or both.

Wines.—Adulterating or selling adulterated wines, knowingly, f $50 to $300 and costs.—Using or counterfeiting private mark, stamp, trade-mark, etc., of wine, f not ex $100 and j not ex 3 mo. Putting adulterated liquors into vessels having private stamp etc., usually affixed by maker of domestic wine with intent to deceive or defraud by the sale thereof, f not ex $100, j 3 to 12 mo, or both.

Witness refusing to take oath or affirmation, when legally called upon, may be committed to prison until he or she shall consent to take such oath or affirmation, and f not ex $20.

REVENUES OF THE STATE.

CHAPTER LIII.

ASSESSMENT AND COLLECTION OF TAXES. *

We have seen from preceding chapters, something of the magnitude and importance of the public works of the State; something of the machinery of its government, and something of the institutions it establishes, fosters and supports. We have also learned of the sources from which a portion of the funds are derived to carry on the government.

It now remains for us to examine more in detail the rules adopted by the State for the purpose of providing itself with the funds necessary to enable its officers and agents to execute the duties with which they are charged.

A tax is a contribution which individuals are required to make for the use or service of the State.

* Most of the revenue of the State is derived by tax as indicated in this chapter. This, however, does not embrace the tolls, received on public works, moneys realized from fines, forfeitures or licenses, nor from specific taxes. But these sums are comparatively insignificant.

Since it is the duty of the government to protect and defend the people in the enjoyment of their property, it is but just that those who have most property should pay the largest tax.

As a basis for taxation, the value of all the real and personal property in the State, except such as the law exempts, is estimated, and a certain percentage of its value is required to be paid as a tax, by the owner, or persons in the possession of such property.

Nearly if not all public property, such as property belonging to the United States, or this State property belonging to the political sub-divisions of the State and used for public purposes; colleges and other institutions of learning, not used with the view to profit; charitable and benevolent institutions, and burying grounds, except such as are held with a view to profit or for the purpose of speculating in the sale thereof; is exempt from taxation. The personal property of each individual not exceeding fifty dollars in value is also exempt from taxation.

As we have seen in another chapter, assessors are required to make out and return to the county auditors, lists and valuations of the taxable property in their respective districts. To enable them to do this, the law requires the owners or persons having possession of property to make out lists thereof and deliver the same to the assessor. See Statutes, Swan and Sayler, 756—For the law concerning taxing of banks and bank stock, railroad, express and telegraph companies, see Swan and Sayler, 763, 766, and 769.

The counties are divided by the commissioners into

districts, in each of which an assessor of real estate is elected by the people, every tenth year.

Each district assessor is required on or before the first Monday of July, every fifth year, (from and after 1870), to return to the county auditor the description and value of each lot or parcel of land in his district, and the names of the parties in whose names the several lots of land in his district have been listed. If the name of the owner of any piece or parcel of land is not known, he must return that fact.

In order that the burden of taxation may be equally distributed, boards of equalization have been established by law.

The county auditor and county commissioners compose the annual county board of equalization of real and personal property. They are required to meet at the auditor's office on the first Wednesday after the third Monday of May, annually, to hear complaints, and equalize the valuation of all real and personal property, money and credits in the county, exclusive of cities of the first and second class.

There is also a special annual board of equalization in cities of the first and second class, composed of the county auditor and six citizens appointed by the city council.

The county auditor, county surveyor and county commissioners, or a majority of them, constitute, every tenth year, a board of equalization, of the real property of their county, with the exception of the real property of cities of the first and second class, which is equalized by a special board provided for by law. They may, every tenth year, raise or reduce the valuation of such tracts and lots as in their opinion have been returned above or below their true relative value, when compared with the other real estate of the county, but they cannot reduce the aggregate value of the lands of the county below that returned by the assessors.

The special board for the equalization of the real property in cities of the first and second class, every tenth year, is composed of the county auditor and six citizens in each of said cities appointed by the city council.

The county auditor is required, on or before the second Monday of October, every tenth year, (from and after 1870), to return to the State auditor, an abstract of the real property in each township in his county, except town lots, with the value thereof.

The State board of equalization consists of the State auditor and a representative from each senatorial district of the State, except the first, which is entitled to three members, who compare the returns from the county auditors and equalize the value of the real property of the State, having due regard to the relative situation, soil, inprovements, and natural and artificial advantages.

Questions.—What is a tax? What is considered as a basis of taxation? What property is exempt from taxation? How are lists of property procured? What is said of district assessors, and what of their duties? For what purpose are boards of equalization established? What officers constitute the annual county board of equalization? When and where do these boards meet, and what are their duties? What is said of special annual boards? What is said of the decennial or ten year boards for counties? For cities? What statement is the county auditor required to make to the State auditor? Who compose the State board of equalization? What are the duties of this board?

CHAPTER LIV.

ASSESSMENT AND COLLECTION OF TAXES, CONTINUED.

The auditor of State is required to transmit to each of the county auditors a statement of the determinations of the State board of eqalization, and to notify them annually of the rates per centum required by the General Assembly to be levied for the payment of the principal and interest of the public debt, for the support of common schools, for defraying the expenses of the State, and for such other purposes as shall be prescribed by law; which rates or per centum shall be levied by the county auditor on the taxable property of each county, on the duplicate, and shall be entered in one column and denominated State taxes.

The county commissioners at their March or at their June session, annually, determine on the amount to be raised for ordinary county purposes, for public buildings, for the support of the poor, and for interest and principal on the county debt. These are denominated county taxes.

The trustees of the several townships in each county on or before the fifteenth day of June, annually, determine the amount necessary to be raised in their townships for ordinary township purposes, for the payment of legal and just claims against such townships, and certify the same to the county auditor who levies the same on the duplicate. These taxes are denominated township taxes.

The council of any municipal corporation is authorized

and required to certify to the auditor of the county on or before the second Monday of June, annually, the percentage by them levied on the real and personal property in their corporation, appraised and returned on the grand levy.

Each board of education, at a regular or special meeting held between the third Monday in April and the first Monday in June of each year, determines by estimate as nearly as practicable, the entire amount of money necessary as a contingent fund to be expended for prolonging the several schools of the district; for the purchase of suitable sites for school houses; for leasing, purchasing, erecting and furnishing school houses; and for all other school expenses, not exceeding seven mills on the dollar of the taxable property of the district, as valued for taxation.

The amount so estimated the board is required to certify, in writing, on or before the first Monday in June in each year, to the auditor of the county to which such district belongs.

The organization of school districts and the duties of school officers are considered in the chapter on Education.

The county auditor after receiving statements of the rates and sums to be levied for the current year in his county, proceeds to levy and apportion the same equitably upon the property listed in the several districts, townships, villages and cities in his county.

The tax lists and duplicates are prepared and arranged in books, by the county auditor, and embrace a complete list or schedule of all the taxable property in his county and the value thereof as equalized and arranged in the form following: Each separate tract of real property in each township in his county, other than town property, shall be contained in a line or lines opposite the name of the owner or owners, arranged in numerical or alphabetical order. The value of the personal property, moneys, credits, investments in bonds, stocks, joint stock companies, or otherwise, of each person, company, or corporation, within each township, shall be set down in a column opposite the name of the owner, person or corporation, in whose name the same is listed; the names of persons in each township, who are not residents of an incorporated town, shall be set down in alphabetical order in one list and the names of persons who are residents of any incorporated town in another list, in alphabetical order.

The county auditor is required, on or before the first day of October, annually, to deliver to the county treasurer a duplicate of taxes required by law to be made out; and it is the duty of the treasurer to collect and receive the taxes and to pay them out in the manner provided by law, to the parties entitled thereto.

The lien of the State for taxes levied for all purposes in each year shall attach to all real property subject to such taxes on the day preceding the second Monday of April annually, and shall continue until such taxes, with any penalty which shall accrue thereon, shall be paid.

All personal property subject to taxation shall be liable to be seized and sold for taxes, and the personal property of any deceased person shall be liable in the hands of any executor or administrator, for any tax due on the same by any testator or intestate, and if the tax on lands shall not be paid, such lands may be advertised and sold, in the manner provided by law, to pay the same.

Questions.—What statements are required to be made by the State auditor to the county auditors? What are denominated State taxes? County taxes, and how are they determined? Township taxes, and how are they determined? What is said of city and village councils? Of boards of education? After receiving statements of rates and sums to be levied, what is the auditor required to do? How are the tax lists and duplicates prepared, and what do they embrace? What is the auditor to do with the duplicate? What is required of the county treasurer? When does a lien attach to lands for the taxes levied thereon? What is said of the lien upon personal property? If the tax levied upon lands be not paid, in what way may payment be enforced?

REAL ESTATE AND PERSONAL PROPERTY.

CHAPTER LV.

REAL ESTATE—DEEDS — POWERS OF ATTORNEY — MORTGAGES.

Real property is that which consists of land, and of all rights and profits arising from and annexed to land, of a permanet, immovable nature.

A deed is a written instrument, under seal, containing an agreement, and which has been delivered by the parties.

A deed of lands is a writing, sealed and delivered, by which lands, tenements, and heraditaments are conveyed.

While a deed to be valid must be delivered, it has been held by the supreme court that "it is not essential to the validity of a deed that it be actually delivered to, or even pass into the hands of the grantee. If delivered to a third person as an *escrow*, it will take effect immediately on the performance of the condition; and if necessary, for the purpose of protecting the grantee against intervening rights, will be held to take effect from the time of the first delivery as an *escrow*."

The statute requires that deeds and mortgages shall be signed and sealed by the grantors, and acknowledged in the presence of two witnesses, who shall attest such signing and sealing, and subscribe their names to such attestation.

Ever since June 1, 1805, by statute, a scrawl seal to a deed has been alike valid as a seal of wax or wafer.

Deeds and other instruments necessary to be acknowledged, may be acknowledged before a judge of the supreme court or of the court of common pleas, a justice of the peace, notary public, mayor or other presiding officer of an incorporated town or city.

Any colonel, lieutenant-colonel, major or adjutant of any regiment or battalion raised in this State, in the service of the United States or of this State, may take acknowledgments of deeds, etc.

Commissioners in other States are appointed by the governor of this State, who may take the acknowledgment of deeds, etc., of lands in this State.

Consuls of the United States resident in a foreign port or country may take the acknowledgment of instruments concerning lands in this State.

Powers of attorney may be given to enable third persons to execute deeds for and in behalf of grantors.

Powers of attorney for the conveyance or incumbrance of lands must be executed and acknowledged in the same manner as deeds; and must be recorded in the office of the recorder of the county in which the lands are situated.

A legal mortgage of lands is described as "a conveyance of lands, by a debtor to his creditor, as a pledge and security for the re-payment of a sum of money borrowed, or performance of a covenant; with a proviso, that such conveyance shall be void on payment of the money and interest on a certain day, or the performance of such covenant by the time appointed, by which the conveyance of the land becomes absolute at law; yet the mortgagor has an equity of redemption, that is, a right in equity on the performance of the agreement within a reasonable time to call for a re-conveyance of the land."

The supreme court of Ohio has decided that "a mortgage of real estate is regarded in equity as a mere security for the performance of its condition of defeasance."

The defeasance here referred to is the condition in the mortgage which, if performed, defeats the operation of the instrument as a deed of conveyance.

The requirements in relation to the execution, acknowledgment and attestation of a mortgage are the same as in case of an absolute deed.

A mortgagee may release a mortgage by entering satisfaction or a receipt for the same, either on the mortgage or on the record of the mortgage.

Deeds and mortgages are valid as between the parties thereto, when executed and delivered. But for the purpose of protecting innocent parties from being defrauded by purchasing lands or receiving mortgages from those who had already sold or mortgaged such lands, the law has provided that a record may be made of such instruments in the office of the recorder of the county. Hence the law provides that mortgages, as to third parties have no effect until delivered to the recorder for record.

All other deeds and instruments for the conveyance or incumbrance of lands are required to be recorded within six months from the date thereof. If not, and a person in good faith purchases the lands at any time thereafter, and before such instrument shall be recorded, the first or unrecorded deed is deemed fraudulent and void as to such subsequent purchaser in good faith.

Instruments for conveying or incumbering real estate in Ohio, may be executed by males who are twenty-one years of age, and by females who are eighteen years of age.

A married woman in order to convey or incumber her interest in real estate must join with her husband in the deed, and the officer taking her acknowledgment must first examine her separate and apart from her husband.

A deed executed by a minor is not void but is valid to vest the title in the grantee until the deed is disaffirmed by such minor after coming of age. Any act manifesting unequivocally the intention to disaffirm, would render the avoidance of the deed effectual; and this may be done at any time before the statute of limitation takes effect.

The confirmation of a minor's deed after coming of full age may be inferred from either an express recognition of the validity of the deed, or from any act done under a knowledge of his rights, which demonstrates his willingness to be bound by the contract; or by continuing, after acquiring such knowledge, to enjoy any benefit, profit or privilege under the contract.

Lapse of time after the age of majority may furnish

evidence of acquiescence, and thus tend to confirm the title, but of itself does not destroy the right to avoid the deed. But if, in the meantime, he has shown a manifest intention to confirm the deed, that, in connection with the lapse of time, though less than twenty-one years, will amount to a confirmation.

Questions.—What is real property? What is a deed? A deed of lands? What is said of the delivery of a deed? Of certain statutory requirements? Of the seal? What officers may take the acknowledgment of deeds and other instruments? Of powers of attorney? What is a mortgage of lands? What has the supreme court of Ohio decided concerning mortgages? What is a defeasance? What formalities are to be observed in the execution of real estate mortgages? How may such mortgage be released? What is said as to the validity of deeds and mortgages between the parties thereto? State the principal object of recording deeds and mortgages. The effect of a failure to record. Who may execute instruments affecting the title to real estate? How may a married woman convey or incumber her interest in lands? What is said of the validity of a minor's deed? How may such deed be disaffirmed? What is said of the confirmation of such deed?

CHAPTER LVI.

OF PERSONAL PROPERTY—TITLE BY DESCENT—DOWER.

Personal property, which consists, in general, of things temporary and movable, may be conveyed without the formality required in the conveyance of real estate. Delivery and acceptance, with the intention that the title pass is sufficient.

Personal property may be mortgaged or pledged as

security for the payment of money or the performance of any legal obligation.

A mortgage of personal property, or chattel mortgage, may be defined as a conveyance or sale of goods, to become an absolute interest if not redeemed at a certain time. [See statutes, Swan and Critchfield, 475; Swan and Sayler, 293.]

If a person die without having disposed of his property, the title to such property vests either in some person or persons, or escheats to the State.

A person who dies without having made a will is called an *intestate*.

The person upon whom the law casts the title of an estate, upon the death of the owner, is called an *heir-at-law*; and the title thus acquired is called title by descent.

The statutes of the State provide for the order in which the title to property shall descend, and indicate who shall be deemed heirs of an estate. [See Swan and Sayler, 304.]

Dower is an estate for life which the law gives the widow in the third part of the lands and tenements of which her husband was seized as an estate of inheritance, at any time during the coverture.

By statute the widow is endowed of one-third part of all the right, title or interest that her husband, at the time of his decease, had in any lands and tenements held by bond, article, lease or other evidence of claim; and she is entitled to remain in the mansion house of her husband, free of charge, for one year after his death, if her dower be not sooner assigned.

An estate of inheritance is one that the heir-at-law of the deceased may inherit.

The wife may also be endowed of certain other estates of the husband. [See Swan and Critchfield, 516.]

Questions.—Of what does personal property consist? What is said of the transfer of the title to personal property? What is a chattel mortgage? What becomes of the title to property, on the death of the owner? Define the word *intestate*. *Heir-at-law*. What is the title inherited by an heir-at-law called? What is dower? Mention what provision is made by statute in relation to dower in lands held by bond, etc.? In relation to the decedent's mansion? What is an estate of inheritance?

DOMESTIC RELATIONS.

CHAPTER LVII.

MARRIAGE, WHO MAY CONTRACT—PROPERTY RIGHTS OF MARRIED WOMEN—LIABILITY OF HUSBAND—TITLE OF THE HUSBAND BY THE CURTESY—APPRENTICES AND SERVANTS.

Male persons of the age of eighteen years, and females of the age of fourteen years, not nearer of kin than first cousins, and not having a husband or wife living, may be joined in marriage: Provided, that males under the age of twenty-one years, and females under the age of eighteen years, shall first obtain the consent of their fathers respectively; or in case of the death or incapacity of their fathers, then of their mothers or guardians.

White persons and Africans are prohibited from inter-marrying. (See chapter on Crimes and Misdemeanors.)

Justices of the peace, duly licensed ministers of the gospel, and the several religious societies, agreeably to their rules and regulations may solemnize marriages.

Previous to persons being joined in marriage, notice

thereof must be published (in the presence of the congregation) on two different days of public worship; the first publication to be at least ten days previous to such marriage, within the county where the female resides; or a license shall be obtained for that purpose, from the probate judge of the county where such female resides. For penalties for violation of marriage laws, see chapter on Crimes and Misdemeanors.

The relations of husband and wife in reference to property are regulated by statute, many of the harsh rules of the common law having been abrogated. The personal property of a woman at her marriage, or that may subsequently be given to her, or be purchased with her means, the wages for her separate labor, or means acquired as damages for a violation of her personal rights, together with the income, increase and profits thereof, remains and continues her separate property, unless and until she permits the husband to reduce the same to his possession, and to treat it as his property.

If a husband desert his wife, or from intemperance or other cause becomes incapaciated or neglects to provide for his family, the wife may in her own name make contracts for her own labor, and the labor of her minor children, and may sue for and collect her own or their earnings; and the court of common pleas has power in such case, on a proper showing, to make an order or judgment, vesting such woman with the rights, privileges, and liabilities of an unmarried woman, as to acquiring, possessing, and disposing of property, real and personal, making contracts and being liable thereon, and suing and being sued in her own name; provided after such judgment the husband shall not be liable upon any contract so made by her in her own name, or for any tort thereafter committed by her.

The real estate of a woman at her marriage, or that which she may subsequently acquire by gift, devise or inheritance, or that may be purchased with her separate means, together with the rents and profits thereof, continues to remain her separate property; and she may make contracts in relation to the improving or leasing of the same, in her own name.

In actions against husband and wife upon any cause existing against her at their marriage, or upon any tort committed by her during coverture, or upon any contract made by her concerning her separate property, her property is liable to be taken to satisfy any judgment therein.

Husbands are entitled to the estate of their deceased wives by the curtesy.

Curtesy or *Courtesy* is defined as, "a life-rent, given by law to the surviving husband, of all his wife's heritage of which she died infeft, if there was a child of the marriage born alive." But by the statutes of Ohio the husband is entitled to the curtesy whether there has been issue born during coverture or not.

The husband, whose duty it is to provide for his family, is liable for necessaries furnished them.

Male children under the age of twenty-one years, and females under the age of eighteen years may be bound to serve as clerks, apprentices or servants until they arrive at those ages respectively.

Orphans and children of parents who fail to provide for them, may be "bound out" by the township trustees. In other cases, the indenture or covenant of service must be signed by the father; or, in case of his death or inability, by the mother or guardian.

The law requires that the indenture or any covenant by which any minor may be bound shall contain, in case of a female bound to service for four years or more, a covenant, on the part of the master or mistress, to teach or cause such minor to be taught to read and write, and also the first four rules of arithmetic; and in case of a male bound to serve five years or more, to read and write, and so much of arithmetic as will include the single rule of three, if such minor can by law, be received into and educated in any common school; and in all cases at the expiration of the term of service, to furnish the minor with a new bible, and at least two suits of common wearing apparel; and all money or property stipulated to be paid by the master or mistress shall be secured to and for the sole use and benefit of the minor.

Orphan or destitute children may be bound to orphan asylums, by the trustees, oversers of the poor, or other proper officers. Parents may also "bind out" their children to orphan asylums.

The several courts of common pleas may grant divorces. *

* The causes for divorce, recognized by the statutes of this State are as follows: 1. When either of the parties had a former wife or husband living, at the time of solemnizing the second marriage. 2. Where either of the parties shall have been willfully absent from the other three years. 3. Adultery. 4. Impotency. 5. Extreme cruelty. 6. Fraudulent contract. 7. Gross neglect of duty. 8. Habitual drunkeness for three years. 9. Imprisonment in States prison or penitentiary for violation of some law of the United States, or of a law of some other State, Territory, or District of Columbia, which if the offence had been committed in this State would be punishable by imprisonment in the penitentiary. Where a divorce has been granted in another State, to a party, the other party, may, for good cause shown, be divorced,.

The court has power to grant alimony to the wife for her sustenance during a petition for divorce, and in case her petition for divorce is granted, she is restored to her separate property, and to her maiden name if she so desires, and allowed such alimony out of her husband's real and personal property, as the court shall think reasonable.

If the husband file a petition for divorce, the wife may file a cross-petition for alimony, with or without a prayer for divorce, setting up in her petition for the relief sought, some of the grounds enumerated in sec. 10, chap. 37 of the Revised Statutes, by Swan and Critchfield.

The court has power, on the petition of the wife, and on proper showing, to grant her a separate maintenance out of her husband's estate, without dissolving the marriage, and may vest in her the power to acquire and dispose of property and to sue and be sued the same as if she were an unmarried woman.

Questions—What persons are deemed competent to contract marriage? Who may solemnize marriages? What is said of notice or license? What is said of the personal property of married women? In case a husband desert his wife or becomes dissipated, what acts may the wife perform in her own name? What order may be made by the court? What is said of the real estate of the wife? Of certain actions against husband and wife? Of title by the curtesy? Of the liability of the husband for necessaries? Of apprentices? What does the law require in the indentures of apprenticeship? What courts have power to grant divorces? What power has the court in regard to the granting of alimony? What is said of a cross-petition? Of the separate maintenance of the wife? Of certain rights with which she may be vested in such case?

---

where the other party has already procured a divorce in some other State, by virtue of which the party obtaining the decree shall have been released from the obligation of the marriage contract, while the same remains binding upon the other party.

SUNDRY MATTERS AFFECTING CIVIL RIGHTS.

CHAPTER LVIII.

THE LAW CONCERNING LIENS.

Bouvier, in his Law Dictionary, has given us an abstract of authorities on the law of liens, arranging the matter methodically, and stating the conclusions of the courts with clearness and brevity.

He says:

"In its most extensive signification, this term includes every case in which real or personal property is charged with the payment of any debt or duty; every such charge being denominated a lien on the property. In a more limited sense it is defined to be a right of detaining the property of another until some claim be satisfied.

"There are two kinds of lien; namely, *particular* and *general*. When a person claims a right to certain property in respect of money or labor expended on such particular property, this is a *particular lien*.

"Liens may arise in three ways: 1st. By express contract. 2d. From implied contract, as from general or particular usage of trade. 3d. By legal relation between the parties, which may be created in three ways; 1. When the law casts an obligation on a party to do a particular act, and in return for which, to secure him payment, it gives him such lien; common carriers and inn-keepers are among this number. 2. When goods are delivered to a tradesman or any other, to expend his labor upon, he is entitled to detain those goods until he is remunerated for the labor which he so expends. 3. When goods have been saved from the perils of the sea, the salvor may detain them until his claim for salvage is satisfied; but in no other case has the finder of goods a lien.

"*General liens* arise in three ways: 1. By the agreement of the parties. 2. By the general usage of trade. 3. By particular usage of trade.

"*How liens may be acquired.*—To create a valid lien, it is essential, 1st. That the party to whom or by whom it is acquired should have the absolute property or ownership of the thing, or, at least, a right to vest it. 2. That the party claiming the lien should have an actual or constructive possession, with the assent of the party against whom the claim is made. 3d. That the lien should arise upon an agreement, express or implied, and not be for a limited or specific purpose inconsistent with the express terms, or the clear extent of the contract, as, for example, when goods are deposited to be delivered to a third person, or to be transferred to another place.

"*The debts or claims to which liens properly attach.*—1st. In general, liens properly attach on liquidated demands, and not on those which sound only in damages; though by an express contract they may attach even in such a case; as, where the goods are to be held as an indemnity against a future contingent claim or damages. 2. The claim for which the lien is asserted, must be due to the party claiming it in his own right, and not merely as agent of a third person. It must be a debt or demand due from the very person for whose benefit the party is acting, and not from a third person, although the goods may be claimed through him.

"*How a lien may be lost.*—1st. It may be waived or lost by any act or agreement between the parties, by which it is surrendered, or becomes inapplicable. 2d. It may also be lost by voluntarily parting with the possession of the goods. But to this rule there are some exceptions; for example, when a factor, by lawful authority, sells the goods of his principal, and parts with the possession under the sale, he is not, by this act, deemed to lose his lien, but it attaches to the proceeds of the sale in the hands of the vendee.

"*The effect of liens.*—In general, the right of the holder of the lien is confined to the mere right of retainer. But when the creditor has made advances on the goods of a factor, he is generally invested with the right to sell. In some cases where the lien would not confer a power to sell, a court of equity would decree it. And courts of admiralty will decree a sale to satisfy maritime liens.

"Judgments rendered in courts of record are generally liens on the real estate of the defendants or parties against whom such judgments are given."

Provision has been made by statute to create a lien

in favor of mechanics and others to enable them to secure what is justly their due, in certain cases.

This lien attaches to the property on account of which the obligation to pay arises. Thus, persons who perform labor or furnish materials or machinery for constructing, altering or repairing any watercraft, or for erecting or repairing any building or appurtenance thereto, by virtue of a contract with the owner thereof, have a lien to secure the payment of the same, and in the case of buildings, upon the lot or land upon which such building stands, provided the owner of the building is the owner of such land; and in case he has only a leasehold interest in the land, such interest is liable to satisfy the lien.

For liens created by statute, and the manner of enforcing them, see Swan and Critchfield, 420, 833; Session Laws of 1871, 107; Session Laws of 1874, 162.

Questions.—What is a lien? How many kinds are there? How do they arise? Give illustrations? What is essential to a valid lien? To what debts or claims do liens attach? How may a lien be lost? What is said of the effect of liens? Of judgments? Of statutory liens?

CHAPTER LIX.

OF WEIGHTS AND MEASURES—PARTITION FENCES.

The law provides how many pounds of grain, dried fruit, coal, vegetables and products shall constitute a bushel: Wheat, 60; rye, 56; shelled corn, 56; corn in ear, 70; oats, 33; clover seed, 62; timothy seed, 45; hemp-seed, 44; millet seed, 50; buckwheat, 50; beans, 60; peas, 60; hominy, 60; Irish potatoes, 60; sweet potatoes, 50; dried peaches, 33; dried apples, 25; flax-seed, 56; barley, 48; malt, 34; Hungarian grass seed, 50; stone coal, 80 for bituminous and 70 for cannel.

A cord of fire-wood consists of 128 cubic feet, *well stowed and packed*.

Apple and potato barrels must be made of seasoned timber, of staves twenty-seven inches in length, when finished, with cut heads of seventeen inches diameter.

The law provides that "all barrels of beef or pork, shall be made of sound, seasoned white oak timber, clear of sap wood, twenty-nine inches in length, when finished, with a cut head of seventeen and a half inches in diameter, tightly bound with strong hoops, one-third of the length thereof, at each end, and when packed and headed up, the outward hoop on each end shall be secured with four nails of suitable size.

"Each barrel of beef or pork put up for exportation in this State shall contain two hundred pounds weight of sound, cleaned, well slaughtered meat, and such only as is well fatted."

Beef is known in market either as "mess beef" or "prime beef"; "mess beef" containing the choicest pieces. Pork is also graded, and is known either as "prime pork," (which is the highest grade) "mess pork" or "navy pork." [See Swan and Sayler, 719.]

A barrel of fish must contain two hundred pounds.

Fences.—The respective owners, or lessees for one or more years, of lands inclosed with fences, are required to keep up and maintain in good repair, all partition fences between their own and the next adjoining inclosures, in equal shares, so long as both parties continue to occupy or improve the same.

Controversies in relation to partition fences are to be decided by the township trustees.

Questions.—Give the weight per bushel of the different grains, fruits and products mentioned in this lesson. What constitutes a cord of fire-wood? How must apple and potato barrels be made? Beef and pork barrels? What is said of the quality and quantity of beef and pork to be packed in each barrel? How are beef and pork graded? How many pounds of fish are required for a barrel? What is said of the keeping up of partition fences? What officers are required to decide controversies respecting partition fences?

CHAPTER LX.

MONEY AND INTEREST.

The parties to any bond, bill, promissory note or other instrument in writing, for the forebearance or payment of money at any future time, may stipulate therein for the payment of interest upon the amount of such bond, bill, note or other instrument of writing, at any rate, not exceeding eight per centum per annum, payable annually. In other cases the rate of interest is six per cent.

Rule for calculating interest.—Suppose the rate of interest to be six per cent. Payments made upon notes or installments before due should be applied to the extinguishment of the principal and such proportion of interest as has accrued upon the principal thus extinguished at the time of the payment. For instance a bond or note is given for the payment of one hundred dollars on or before the termination of one year, with interest. At the end of six months a payment of fifty-one dollars and fifty cents is made. This is not applied to sink the balance of the principal to forty-eight dollars and fifty cents, but the one dollar and fifty cents is applied to the interest of fifty dollars for six months, and fifty dollars to sink so much of the principal. At the end of the year there will be due fifty dollars of principal and the interest on that fifty dollars for one year.

The statute fixing the rate of interest is not an act of usury, technically so-called. It does not avoid the contract, except as to the excess of interest over the lawful rate.

Contracts for interest made in other States, when it is sought to enforce them in this State, must be governed by the law of the State where the contract was made—the validity of the agreement depending upon the *lex loci* of the contract.

Questions—What is said of the rate of interest allowable in Ohio? What is the rule for calculating interest? Give an illustration? What is the effect of a contract for excessive interest? What is said of contracts for interest made in other States?

CHAPTER LXI.

APPROPRIATION OF PRIVATE PROPERTY TO PUBLIC USE—EMINENT DOMAIN.

Provision is made by law by which the property of others may be appropriated to the use of the public.

The constitution provides as follows: "Private property shall ever be held inviolate, but subservient to the public welfare. When taken in time of war or other public exigency, imperatively requiring its immediate seizure, or for the purpose of making or repairing roads, which shall be open to the public without charge, a compensation shall be made to the owner in money; and in all other cases where private property shall be taken for public use, a compensation therefor shall first be made in money, or first secured by a deposit of money, and such compensation shall be assessed by a jury, without deduction for benefits to any property of the owner."

The interests of individuals in property are traceable to the government; and in this country the aggregate body of the people in their sovereign capacity constitute the government. It is true that the government grants to individuals the right to take and appropriate estates as their own; and yet the doctrine has always been recognized that the *eminent domain*, the right which the government retains over the estates of individuals, is a sufficient warrant for resuming such estates for public use.

The title to much of the lands in this country has been

derived from the Federal government and not from the State; and it would therefore seem that the Federal rather than the State government would be justified in the exercise of the power of *eminent domain*. But inasmuch as under our somewhat anomalous or at least peculiar system, each State is charged with the protection of its citizens in their persons and property, it has been held that the character of sovereignty in the State necessary to enable it to discharge its functions properly in that respect, requires that the power of *eminent domain* shall pertain to and reside in the State government. This being so, it will be seen that the right is founded more in the necessity growing out of our relations to each other and to society than of a mere implied reservation in the grantor, where the government grants the estate.

Eminent domain may defined as the inherent right necessarily resting in every sovereignty to control and regulate the relative rights of individuals where those rights are of a public nature and pertain to its citizens in common. This being so, no constitutional provision is necessary to give it force. The power is not born of written constitutions but is usually limited by them. It therefore follows that the people, through their representatives are to determine the question as to the propriety and expediency of exercising this right.

In the case of Giesy *vs.* C. W. & Z. R. R. Co., 4 Ohio State Reports, the supreme court held as follows, in relation to the power of eminent domain:

"It may be used to appropriate lands for a public highway of any kind, and this whether the road is built and owned by the public or by a corporation as a public instrumentality, provided it is kept open for public use as a matter of right, or, according to the nature of the work, the corporation is made a common carrier of goods or of passengers.

"It may be exercised directly or indirectly by the General Assembly, without the intervention of the judiciary, except the determining the amount of compensation. But the courts possess full power to determine its proper limit, and to prevent abuses in its exercise.

"The power rests upon necessity, and can only be exercised where such necessity exists. But this necessity relates rather to the nature of the property, and the uses to which it is applied, than to the exigencies of the particular case; and it is no objection to the exercise of the power, that lands, equally feasible, could be obtained by purchase.

"Only such interest as will answer the public wants can be taken; and it can be held only so long as it is used by the public, and cannot be diverted to any other purpose."

Questions.—What provision is made in the State constitution relative to the taking of private property for public use? To what source are the property interests of individuals traceable? What right does the government retain over the estates of individuals? What is said of the exercise of the power of eminent domain by the Federal and State governments?

CHAPTER LXII.

SALARIES OF STATE OFFICERS.

The several officers herein named receive for their services the following sums annually: Governor, $4,000; lieutenant-governor, $800; judges of the supreme court, each, $3,000; judges of the common pleas courts, each, $2,500; secretary of state, $2,000; treasurer of state, $3,000; auditor of state, $3,000; attorney-general, $1,500, and three per centum on all collections made by him for the State; *provided*, the aggregate amount of his compensation including said per centum, shall not exceed $2,000 per annum, during the term of his office; members of the board of public works, each, $800 and no more, in the form of traveling expenses or otherwise; the comptroller of the treasury, $1,700; state librarian, $1,500; state commissioner of common schools, $2,000.

Officers of the penitentiary receive the following salaries: Warden, $2,000; deputy warden, $1,800; clerk, $1,500; assistant clerk, in the discretion of the board of directors, not exceeding $1,000; matron, $800; steward, $1,500; physician, $800; chaplain, $1,500. Other officers of the penitentiary are paid from $45 to $75 per month.

Officers of the benevolent institutions are paid from $300 to $1,200 per annum.

Members of the General Assembly receive, each, five dollars per day, during their attendance at the General Assembly, and also the sum of three dollars for every twenty-five miles distance, by the most direct route of public travel from their place of residence, in traveling to and from the seat of government.

The clerks and sergeants-at-arms of the General Assembly receive $5 per day, for each day's attendance.

The several clerks in the different departments of the State government receive from $400 to $800 per annum.

The clerk of the supreme court, like many other officers, receives, in lieu of a regular salary, fees for services rendered. These fees are fixed by statute.

[The proper questions to the preceding chapter will be readily suggested to the teacher.]

GOVERNMENT OF THE UNITED STATES.

CHAPTER I.

COLONIAL GOVERNMENTS—GOVERNMENT UNDER THE ARTICLES OF CONFEDERATION — ORGANIZATION OF THE FEDERAL GOVERNMENT.

In the early history of this country the people were subjects of the British Empire. Extensive grants of territory were conferred upon individuals and companies. Some of these grants conferred certain powers of government. Out of these grants colonies were organized with charters specifying what governmental powers might be exercised. They authorized the establishment of legislatures to make laws for the government of the people, provided such laws should not conflict with the laws of the British Parliament.

Governors for the colonies were appointed by the King of England, in whom was vested executive authority.

The colonies, while subject to Great Britain, were entirely independent of each other.

In course of time the British government became exacting and oppressive towards the colonies, denying them many of the privileges that had been granted by their charters.

In 1765, at the request of the Massachusetts legislature, the different colonies sent representatives, or *delegates*, to meet in convention to counsel together concerning their difficulties with the British government. In the same year delegates from nine colonies met in New York, and agreed upon and signed petitions and memorials representing their grounds of complaint, and forwarded them to the King.

September 5, 1774, delegates from eleven of the colonies met at Philadelphia. This body was called the Continental Congress. It adjourned in October, to meet again in May, 1775. Various measures were adopted designed to protect the people against the encroachments of the mother country, and on the 4th of July, 1776, Congress declared the colonies to be free and independent States.

Thus far, no provision had been made for incorporating the States into one nation for the purposes of government; but believing it to be necessary for their mutual protection and safety, in November, 1776, a plan of union was agreed upon. This plan was set out in a writing called, "Articles of Confederation and perpetual union between the States," and was to become operative, that is, go into effect, when adopted by the Legislatures of all the States.

In 1778, the articles were adopted by eleven of the States; in 1779, by one, and by the thirteenth and last, in

1781. So that on the 23d of March, 1781, the new government went into operation, under the name of the United States of America.

It was soon found that the Articles of Confederation did not confer sufficient power upon the National Government, to make it effective. Its powers were vested in Congress; and no provision had been made for an executive or a judicial department. It could pass laws but could not enforce them. It could determine how many men and how much money each State should furnish to carry on the war, but it was left for the States to execute the law. If they refused, there was no law to compel them to comply. To defray the expenses of the war, Congress borrowed large sums of money; several millions of which was from Holland and France.

Another difficulty arose from the fact that different States enacted laws giving their own citizens undue advantages over the citizens of other States.

To enable the National Government to control, in needful cases, the action of the States, it was found necessary to confer greater powers upon it. So in May, 1787, delegates chosen by all the States, except Rhode Island, assembled at Philadelphia, and adopted our present constitution. This was submitted to the people of the States for their approval.

The people chose delegates in each State to attend State conventions, with power to approve or reject the proposed constitution. These conventions approved the constitution, and thus our present government was established.

The constitution of the United States may be said to be an agreement of the different States with each other, as to the forms and powers of the national government. It confers certain powers of government and control over the States and the people of the United States. Hence we refer to the constitution and the government as the Federal constitution, or the Federal Government.

Questions.—Of what government were the people of this country formerly subjects? What is said of the organization of colonies? Who appointed the governors? What action was taken by the colonies in 1765? In 1774? In 1776? When were the Articles of Confederation adopted? What powers had the government under the Articles of Confederation? What was the occasion for a change in the government? How and when was this change effected? What is said of the constitution of the United States?

CHAPTER II.

EXECUTIVE DEPARTMENT OF THE GOVERNMENT OF THE UNITED STATES—THE DIFFERENT SECRETARIES AND THEIR DUTIES.

The Executive department of the Government is vested in the President. The duties of the President and Vice President are similar to those of the governor and lieutenant-governor of a State. The President appoints the officers necessary to assist him in executing the laws.

Most of the executive business is done through departments; and each department has a head officer called a secretary.

The Secretary of State performs for the National Government duties similar to those performed by the State secretaries for the States; and in addition thereto, he has charge of our affairs with foreign nations, and gives directions under the President, to our foreign ministers and consuls.

The Secretary of the Treasury has charge of and conducts the financial affairs of the Government. Amongst other things, it is his duty to attend to the collection of funds for the support of the Government; to make out and report to Congress estimates of the public revenues and expenses, and to inform that body what appropriations will be needed for the use of the Government.

The Secretary of War has charge of the Military Department.

The Secretary of the Navy has the charge of the business relating to the Navy.

The Attorney-General is the legal adviser of the President and heads of the various Departments, and prosecutes suits in the Supreme Court of the United States.

The Postmaster-General has the general supervision of post offices, and of the carrying and distributing of the mails.

The Secretary of the Interior has charge of the Indian, land, pension, and patent matters.

The heads of these several Departments constitute the President's Cabinet, and are his counsellors and advisers.

Questions—In whom is the Executive department of the United States vested? Does the President execute the laws in person? How does he execute them? Name the chief department officers. What are the duties of each?

CHAPTER III.

LEGISLATIVE DEPARTMENT OF THE GOVERNMENT OF THE UNITED STATES.

The Legislative Department is vested in Congress, consisting of two bodies: a senate and house of representatives.

The senate has two members from each State who are elected for six years.

The Vice-President is the presiding officer of the senate.

The advice and consent of the senate is necessary for the appointment of many of the officers of the Government.

When charges are preferred against certain officers of the United States, the senate tries them; and when sitting for that purpose, is a court of impeachment. The Chief Justice of the Supreme Court presides on such occasions.

In matters of legislation, the proceedings of the two houses of Congress are similar to those of the two branches of the General Assembly. The members of the house of representatives hold their offices for two years. The States are divided into districts, and a member is elected in each district.

The powers of Congress are delegated to it by the constitution; and in this respect it differs from the State Legislatures. The State constitutions prescribe and indicate what the Legislatures may not do; the Federal constitution declares what Congress may do. Hence, in determining whether an act of Congress is constitutional, the question is, "Does the constitution authorize the act?"—and in determining whether an act of a State Legislature is constitutional, the question is, "Does the constitution forbid it?" But by the constitution of Ohio, it is provided "that all powers, not hereby delegated, remain with the people;" and it was held by the supreme court, in 1st Ohio State Reports, page 77, that any act passed by the General Assembly, not falling fairly within the scope of legislative authority, is as clearly void as though expressly prohibited.

Questions.—In what body is the Legislative department of the Government vested? How many members has the senate? Mention some of the duties of the senate, not pertaining to the ordinary matters of legislation? How are members of the house elected? How long is their term of office? What is said of the powers of Congress? In what respect do the powers of Congress differ from the powers of State Legislatures? What is the test of the constitutionality of an act? What provision is made by the constitution of Ohio with reference to certain powers?

CHAPTER IV.

GOVERNMENT OF THE UNITED STATES, CONTINUED—THE JUDICIAL DEPARTMENT—SALARIES OF OFFICERS.

The Federal constitution provides that the Judicial power of the United States shall be vested in one Supreme Court, and such inferior courts as Congress may, from time to time, establish. It also enumerates the duties and powers of these courts.

The Supreme Court consists of nine members.

The United States is divided into ten circuits, and a judge is appointed in each circuit. The circuit courts revise the decisions of the district courts, and in addition to certain civil causes they may try, they have jurisdiction for the trial of the highest crimes against the United States. When a justice of the Supreme Court of the United States is present at a circuit court, he presides. The judge of a district sometimes sits with the circuit judge, in which case the circuit judge presides.

District courts are established throughout the United States. In each State there is at least one district court. This court has jurisdiction in admiralty, bankruptcy, and many other cases. It also has jurisdiction over offenses against the laws of the United States.

In addition to these, Congress has established a court of claims, for the adjudication of claims against the Government.

The President of the United States receives an annual salary of $50,000; the Vice President, $8,000; Cabinet officers, $8,000 each; Envoys Extraordinary and Ministers Plenipotentiary, from $12,000 to $17,500; Ministers Resident in foreign countries, from $7,500 to $12,000; Ministers Resident and Consuls General, $4,000 to $7,000; members of Congress, $5,000, and mileage at twenty cents per mile each way, to and from Washington.

Questions.—What provision is made in the constitution for the establishment of courts? Of how many members is the Supreme Court composed? How many circuit courts are there in the United States? What is said of the jurisdiction of circuit courts? What judge presides in the circiut court? What is said of the establishment of district courts? Of their jurisdiction? Of the court of claims? What salary does the President of the United States receive? The Vice President? Cabinet officers? Envoys Extraordinary and Ministers Plenipotentiary? Ministers Resident and Consuls General? Members of Congress?

INDEX.

[The reference figures are to the pages.]

www.ingramcontent.com/pod-product-compliance
Lightning Source LLC
LaVergne TN
LVHW010251110826
845151LV00004B/1446

9781425522377